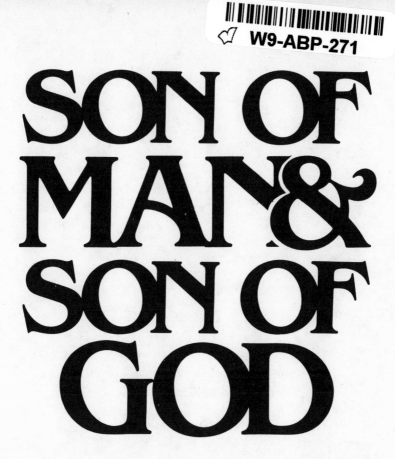

SON OF MAN& SON OF GOD

A New Language for Faith

JOHN C. DWYER

PAULIST PRESS
New York/Ramsey

Library of Congress
Catalog Card Number: 82-60754

ISBN: 0-8091-2505-6

Published by Paulist Press
545 Island Road, Ramsey, N.J. 07446

Printed and bound in the
United States of America

232.

Contents

Introduction

1.1 A Man of Mystery

Almost twenty centuries ago there lived a man whose life and death were marked by strange and sometimes shocking paradox. He lived in an insignificant land which was little more than a backwater of the ancient world, firmly under the control of Rome but without any influence on the powerful currents which emanated from that distant seat of empire. And yet, this man stood at the beginning of a movement which conquered Rome and her empire, and which became the dominant factor in the emergence of a new culture and, ultimately, in the creation of that complex reality which we call "the Western world." And even today, when much of the terrain gained by this movement seems to have been lost, two facts must be kept in mind: first, those who in one form or other claim to follow this man make up more than one quarter of the billions who live on this planet today; second, the very ideologies which compete both in the East and the West with the movement which began with this man themselves rest on a kind of vision and hope which would be incomprehensible without him.

Historical anomalies aside, there was a strangeness about the man himself. As far as we can judge, he spoke with simplicity and power, and yet he was constantly misinterpreted and misunderstood by those who were closest to him. Apparently he had an attractive personality and would be called today "magnetic" or "charismatic." It seems that he inspired loyalty and dedication in those who followed him, but at the end of his life, the

1

loyal following vanished, and he died, deserted by his friends and abandoned by all. His death itself was appalling, not simply in its brutality but in its senselessness. He did not die as a martyr to a noble cause, but as the victim of a stupid, meaningless act of cruelty which accomplished nothing, even for those who perpetrated it.

And there was a strangeness about this man's purpose in life and about the meaning of his words and actions. He is revered today by millions as a religious founder and as the most important religious leader of all time. But it is obvious that the religious leadership of his own people rejected him, and a careful, critical reading of the earliest writings of his followers has made another fact quite clear, although it is a fact so unexpected that it seems to defy comprehension. This man was rejected by the religious leadership of his people not because of their warped and twisted *mis*understanding of religion but because they quite correctly saw something in the words and deportment of this man which constituted a threat, not only to their religious leadership, but to religious doctrine, religious tradition, religious law—in fact, to religion itself and to the conception of God and man for which it stands.

This man is, of course, Jesus, and this book is about him. He is as much a man of mystery today as he was in his lifetime, and the misunderstanding that dogged his steps during life did not come to an end with his death. Even in his own lifetime people tried to penetrate his mystery by relating him to the one they called "God." They called him "Son of God," "Word of God," "Anointed of God," but in death as in life he seemed to elude these attempts to grasp him and hold him. Three hundred years after he died, his followers decided that they could do justice to his mystery only by unequivocally calling him "God," and increasingly, in the sixteen hundred years that separate us from this event—the first ecumenical council at Nicaea—Christians have tended to see in this confession of the "divinity" of

Jesus the soul and substance of their faith. As was to be expected, those who reject Christianity and believe that they hate (or pity) this man Jesus feel duty-bound to reject Nicaea's solution. For them, to call Jesus "God" is to claim too much, and to raise to the divine state this man who so obviously shares our pain and suffering is an intolerable affront, if not to God, at least to our own sense of reality and truth.

For over a hundred years, the confession "Jesus Christ is God" has been a test of orthodoxy, zealously applied by many Christians to those inside and outside their own churches, in the firm belief that they had, in this formula, a diagnostic tool for distinguishing authentic Christian faith from counterfeit forms. And it is this which leads us to the strangest of all the paradoxes about Jesus (and the one which can shed more light on his mystery than any of the others)—the statement that "Jesus Christ is God" is worse than useless as a test of orthodoxy, and, at least very often, rests on assumptions which pose a most serious threat to genuine faith. But the surprising part of the paradox is still to come: the affirmation of the divinity of Jesus poses a threat to faith, not because it exalts Jesus beyond due measure or claims for him an honor to which he is not entitled. The affirmation poses a threat to faith because it ignores what is really unique in Jesus. Under the pretense of giving Jesus the highest honor possible, in reality it forces him to conform to religious conceptions and expectations which are at best limited and, more often, the antithesis of genuine faith. The affirmation threatens faith precisely because, in its formal correctness, it puts at our disposal a clever and effective way of domesticating Jesus and depriving him of the power to criticize our actions and our thoughts, our pretentious claims to ultimacy and the deep misunderstanding of ourselves and of God on which these claims are based.

The affirmation that "Jesus Christ is God" is dangerous in the extreme because of the tacit assumption on which it is based—*the assumption that we know what the word "God" means and then show honor and reverence to Jesus by conferring this title on him.* It is the contention of this book that this assumption is ungrounded and must be rejected by anyone who takes Jesus' word and work seriously. We do not honor Jesus by calling him God.[1] Rather, *it is in and through Jesus that we discover what the word "God" means.* Without Jesus and apart from him, the word "God" is a demand, a hope, a promise and a dream, which human beings have often enough filled with the most questionable content; the pantheon is full of cruel and vindictive "gods" whom we have created in our own image and likeness.[2] In Jesus, the real God is revealed and it is the conviction that this claim is true which gives to Christian faith its unique and distinctive character.

The point being made here is elusive, and, at least to many Christians, shocking. Because of this it cannot be emphasized too strongly that the problem in affirming the "divinity" of Jesus is not that such a statement goes too far; on the contrary, it does not go nearly far enough. The problem is not that such a statement is too strong; on the contrary, it is far too timid and restrained. And for this reason, the affirmation of the "divinity" of Jesus is not the sum and substance of Christian faith, but is rather likely to be a dangerous distortion of faith which confuses the real issue and conceals the mystery of Jesus.

The New Testament makes it clear that simply identifying Jesus with God cannot do justice to the depth and uniqueness of their relationship, but the oldest strata of the Synoptic tradition do characterize this relationship in a way which can illuminate the mystery. Since the rethinking of the mystery of Jesus is the work of this book, it will be appropriate at this point in the introduction to state in preliminary form how the New Testament characterizes his relationship with God. For now it will be enough to enumerate three facts; in a later chapter these facts can be examined in some detail and conclusions can be drawn.

The first fact is this: the man Jesus spoke and acted in such a way that the people who looked at what he did and listened to what he said discovered who God really was.[3] Incidentally, men and women have continued to make this discovery up to the present day, and to make this discovery is to believe in God and in Jesus. Second, Jesus made God known in a definitive and final way which could not be surpassed. Even a cursory reading of the New Testament makes it clear that for those who wrote it, God, the real God, can be known only in and through the mediation of Jesus.[4] Jesus reveals God *definitively,* and this is rooted in the third fact: Jesus did not simply talk about God or point to him; he made God *present* and he made God *real.* He engaged and implicated God in all that he did. Without him, God is, at best, the object of hope and longing. With him, God is present in power.

1.2 Theology, Faith and the Knowledge of God

The question of Jesus is the question of God, in a far deeper sense than is usually accorded these words. This means that in rethinking the mystery of Jesus we will be striving to know God—or, in other words, we will be doing theology. Now a book which claims to do theology confronts the reader with certain demands and challenges which other books do not, and this is the appropriate place to indicate what I mean by the word "theology."

Theology is not a substitute for faith. Above all, it is not an intellectual pastime for those who cannot be satisfied with simple faith. To view it in this light is to make of faith a substitute for or an alternative to critical intelligence, and this represents a profound misunderstanding. Apart from the word "God," perhaps no other element of the religious vocabulary is as consistently misunderstood as "faith." This is particularly true in English, where "believe" is the only verbal form available, and "faith" means, at least to many, an assent which is based on feeling or wishful thinking and which is therefore particularly appropriate for those who cannot cope with the realities of life. But this is merely a parody of faith. Faith is not the act of mortifying the intelligence; it is an act of *knowledge,* and like all real knowledge, it is *critical* in the proper sense of the word. Far from despising or circumventing intelligence, faith will strive to touch and transform the lives of believers by making them *more intelligent* (and it is in doing this that faith plays a role in our moral lives).[5] Faith will make believers more alert to the presence of God, so that they may understand who God really is, draw the right conclusions about God's words and acts, and achieve real freedom by acting responsibly in the presence of this God. *Theology* is the attempt to cultivate this alertness, this understanding, this reasonable reflection and this responsible freedom. Theology does not compete with faith; it is rather a continuation or prolongation of faith.[6] Because faith is knowledge, it must always strive for greater scope and depth; if it does not, it will wither and die. Real faith leads to theology and it is from faith that theology derives its power and purpose. Faith is the motive for doing theology and it is its justification. This book invites the reader to do theology precisely so that faith may be served.

1.21 Since theology is the attempt to know God, words are important to the theologian. We can't understand anything without words (although sometimes the role played by words is indirect, as we will see), and unless the words we use are accurate, understanding will be only partial and limited. Careless language is a symptom of careless thought; this in turn is a symptom of carelessness about reality—the reality of God, the world and ourselves—and this is something the theologian cannot afford.[7]

In all of this it is well to remember that words are not merely *signs* that we have understood something or someone.

The relationship is much more essential: understanding *comes to be* in speech, and this is particularly significant when we strive to understand God.[8] This is true for a very paradoxical reason: it is in what we *cannot* say about God and it is in our *silence* before him that we really know him.[9] Such a silence is not empty, and it is not constituted by the absence of words; it is a filled silence and it is constituted by the presence of a mystery which words cannot comprehend, but which will not manifest itself without the mediation of words.[10] The experienced inadequacy of the most carefully chosen word is the sign of the presence of the "high and holy One" whose thoughts and ways are not our own. Respect for this mystery impels theologians to be exact in the use of words because they know that it is through words that the knowledge of God comes into being, and that it is through words, in prayer, worship and preaching, that the knowledge of God reaches out to touch and transform all of human life.[11]

1.3 The Only Question

Because Jesus *defines* God, there is only one *theo*logical[12] question in the strict sense: Who is Jesus Christ? The word "Jesus" in this question refers to a man who died a little less than twenty centuries ago. The word "Christ" is more difficult, because it is more than a name, more even than a title.[13] To call Jesus the Christ is to state that *Jesus himself* (and not merely his influence) belongs to the present and not solely to the past. To call Jesus the Christ is to state that the human life which had a beginning and an end *there and then* has an essential meaning for human beings in all times and places. To call Jesus the Christ is to affirm that Jesus lives and that his life is a continual offer of new and authentic existence to men and women as long as our race endures. To call Jesus the Christ is to affirm that in him we can live in joy and die in peace, because even the destruction of all earthly hope is not an end but a beginning.[14]

1.31 Can this almost incredible claim be verified? Many answer that it can be verified by faith and by faith alone, but this answer is, at best, inadequate, and at worst it equates faith with an assent for which there is no evidence. Real faith is a response to God, precisely as one who is acting *now* in our lives. To argue that it is through faith that we know that Jesus is the Christ is simply to postpone the real question: What is God doing in our lives in such a way that we can experience it and respond to it?

This question makes great demands on faith because it makes the *experience* of God a necessary condition for faith.[15] Faith is not the passive acknowledgement that *others* have had an experience of God. Faith is the assertion that, with all due allowance for "seeing in a mirror, darkly," nevertheless *I have seen God.*[16] Faith is the assertion that God lives because Jesus does and that *I have experienced the presence of the Lord.* But what is the nature of this experience?

1.32 There are two elements or components in the experience from which faith springs. The first is an experience of *change* or transformation in one's life. The material conditions in which we live our lives remain the same, but the ultimate and proximate goals of life are seen clearly, and in the light of this vision nothing remains the same. We find peace in the midst of turmoil. Fear and anxiety, while not banished, lose their power to threaten and destroy. In terms of an older tradition, our lives are no longer under the control of sin but are now under the power of grace. In more modern terms, we escape from a fragmented existence and find authentic existence, a truly human life. There are always strong emotional components in such an experience, but note carefully that a truly human emotion is not an irrational feeling or an indefinable "high": it is the experience of the beauty, the charm, the attractiveness of some part of reality which has revealed itself to us. In later chapters we will have more to say about the nature of this experience, about its sources and about the necessity of subjecting it to criticism. For the moment we might define it in good New Testament terms as the experience of that peace which the world cannot give.

There is a second element needed if we are to experience that Jesus is the Christ or (to say the same thing in other words) that Jesus was raised from the dead and lives: we experience this peace which the world cannot give through contact with the unique person of Jesus. To call Jesus the Christ is to state that this has happened in one's own life and can happen in the lives of others. But this is a strange and extraordinary statement— one which suffers under great inner tension—and in making it, we strain language to the breaking point and beyond. For we are stating that an individual and limited event, confined to a definite number of years and to a small geographical area, is of absolute significance for all human beings who have ever lived or ever will. The event in which we experience that Jesus is the Christ shares the inner tension of the confession: it bridges the past and the present and moves from the unique historical reality of Jesus of Nazareth to the universal meaning of Jesus as the Christ.[17]

1.4 The Mystery of Language

What is the event in which I experience the personal reality of Jesus? This is not only an important preliminary question for Christology; what is at stake is the very possibility of faith and therefore of Christian existence. How is it possible to conceive of the event in which I contact Jesus in his historical uniqueness and in which at the same time he reveals himself as the one who is of absolute significance for my life and for the lives of all human beings? We can approach this mystery by pondering another—the mystery of the words we human beings speak to each other, the mystery of their power to create and to reveal, to mediate between independent selves and make two persons truly present to each other.

Not all words we speak are creative and revealing. Much of our speech is trivial and banal, and some of it is destructive; some of our speech merely attaches tags or labels to things so we may make use of them and some of our speech manipulates other persons so that we may make use of them. But at times we speak the right word to another. We know this because we have done it for others and they have done it for us and we have been amazed at the power of these words which we have spoken and which we have heard. Such words open up a whole new world; they reveal us to ourselves, and they realize and actuate possibilities of personal existence which were only potential and dormant. It is in hearkening to the creative word spoken by another that I *come to be* a self, a person, and this is the deepest meaning of the social character of human existence.[18]

Words have this power because they are not just pointers, tags or labels. The word, in the sense used here, is the vehicle or medium through which I reveal myself to another and accept the revelation of the other. It is through the word, spoken and heard, that we *meet* one another and do not merely impinge on one another. These words which I speak to another are a direct extension of my own person, my own self.[19] Through the mediation of this word *I* contact, touch, affect the other. Such words are not just things which I use and from which I can distance myself; they are extensions and prolongations of myself. I am present in them and they mediate my personal presence to others. The truth of my word is the truth of my *self.*

This mysterious character of some of the words which we speak is so important for the encounter with Jesus Christ that it is essential to distinguish these words which we speak *to* one another from other very good and useful words which we speak *about* the world and about the human situation. Some great words have been spoken and written with the intention that others will ponder them and act more humanly because of them. Such words create areas or domains of truth into which people of a later age can move. They offer proposals, models of reality, which listeners and readers are urged to act upon and to pass on to later generations. Such words mediate the wisdom of the past and they create a culture which to some degree transcends the limitations of time. They are of vital importance for all of us, corporately and individually, but *they are not the words which are under discussion here.* The distinctively human word is always the word of *address*—the word which I speak to another person from whom I await a response. To some degree each of these words is a sign of respect and of love, and it is from this that they derive their creative power.

The word which we speak to another and which fashions our distinctively human way of being with each other is itself mediated in a variety of ways. The inner word of thought is mediated by the sounds which embody that thought in a given language. Our words to another can be mediated by being written, and it is even possible for a third party to communicate them to the one for whom they are destined. In these cases the word remains my word; the medium or vehicle through which it is passed on does not stop it from being my word but rather makes it possible for my word to reach into a new situation, makes it possible for me to be present in a place from which I would otherwise be absent.[20]

(Perhaps it would be more accurate to say that when my word is mediated to another, either in writing or through a third person, it *can* remain my word—that is, the mere fact of mediation does not *necessarily* alter it and prevent it from being my word. However, the mediation of my word is something over which I will have to keep careful watch. If my word is mediated carelessly or inaccurately, it may cease to be my word. It might become the word of some other person, or it might come to be something quite different from a personal word and become an impersonal statement or directive. It will only be my word to the extent that it remains an extension or prolongation of my own person and to the extent that those to whom it is addressed can find me in it.)[21]

1.5   Jesus and His Word

What is said here about the human word which we address to one another was eminently true of the word of Jesus which he spoke in the years preceding his death. We will look at this in more detail later on, but even a cursory reading of the New Testament will justify the following summary: it was through Jesus' word that he was present to others as one who was *for* them. It was through his word that he brought them the good news of who God really is, the good news of the *real* God. It was through his word that Jesus brought to his hearers real life and true freedom. It was his power to speak this kind of word which constitutes the historical uniqueness of Jesus: he spoke as no man ever spoke; he had the words of eternal life; he taught "with authority" and not as the scribes and Pharisees did. But he had his authority not because he claimed it by some right or because he had been commissioned by the religious leadership of his people.[22] He had authority because he made God real, made God *happen,* and the words he spoke were the instruments he used. His word was not "outside" him and he did not distance himself from it. His word was an extension or prolongation of his concrete historical reality. He is "in" his word, and through this presence he touches all those who hear his word and hearken to it. If "sacrament" means "a sign of the very presence of God which in some way can be touched by our senses" then the word of Jesus is in the fullest sense a sacrament (and the presence and power of Jesus in what are more traditionally called sacraments should be understood this way).[23]

1.51   And now we turn to a fact which is mysterious and striking but which a critical reading of the New Testament makes incontrovertibly clear: Jesus died but *his word to others did not stop with his death.* The word in which Jesus made God real, the word in which he revealed to his hearers both who God really was and who they themselves really were, *continued to be spoken as his word,* and in ever new circumstances it continued to create both life and freedom. Note carefully what is being asserted here: it is *not* simply that Jesus' word *about* life and death, about people and things and values, was handed on. There is nothing very unusual about such words being passed on. The words of Socrates and Confucius, of Julius Caesar, Thomas Aquinas and Karl Marx have been handed on in this way, and through these words the men in question have influenced civilization and transformed the world for centuries after their deaths. But the mysterious thing which happened to Jesus' word is something qualitatively different. After his death, his word continues to be spoken, not as a message which he originated and which then comes to enjoy a certain independence of him, but rather as *his word of address to us,* as a word which *he still speaks.*[24]

It might seem that to make this kind of statement we would have to assume that Jesus rose from the dead, but I believe that the argument should move in precisely the opposite direction: it is because his word continues to be spoken and heard as *his word* that we know that Jesus who died did not stay dead but now lives. The resurrection means far more than the resuscitation of a dead person; it means quite simply that Jesus lives, and this is far too important a fact to be accepted on hearsay.[25]

But what does it mean to say that Jesus' word continues to be spoken *as his word*? What is there about this word which demands more than the acknowledgement that Jesus, who lived and died long ago, commented on God, the world, and the human situation in a way which is worth pondering today? Is it possible to describe the experience of a living and personal word? What is it that differentiates such a personal word from all of the impersonal words which we read and hear and speak? To answer this question will be to describe the most fundamental experience of the Christian—the experience which is the call to faith and the immediate ground and motive of faith.[26] Although the phrase can have many other meanings, I believe that it would be proper to call this experience simply *the Christian experience.*

1.6 The Experience of Jesus' Living Word

The Christian experience is, first of all, the hearing of a word which is not a word *about* God, or the world, or ourselves, but rather a word in which we are *addressed*—a word which is spoken *to* us. Words which are *about* persons and things serve many practical purposes. Such words propose models which may be useful and even good both for acting and for being. They make us think. In fact, we could describe them in general terms by saying that they create *ideas* which are worth examining and, after examination, possibly worth acting upon. But words of address, words which are spoken *to* us, create not ideas but *life.* (This assumes that the words in question are right and good—if they are neither, they may threaten or to some degree destroy life.) The right words which are spoken to us are *healing* words—they create wholeness and with it the possibility of authentic and genuine existence.[27] When such words are spoken to us, we realize that they are the words we have been waiting for and that without being consciously aware of it, we have always been listening for these words. We begin to see that essentially, almost by definition, we are the people who are *waiting for, listening for* this kind of word.

This word of address, this word which is spoken to us, can be characterized in two ways which are seemingly quite differ-

ent, if not contradictory: the word of address is, on the one
hand, a word of acceptance and affirmation, and therefore of
love, while on the other hand it is a word which *lays claim to us*
and makes demands which we cannot evade through facile logic
and clever casuistry.[28] For each of us the experience is the same
in this respect: the word addresses *me* and not the generality of
mankind. But strangely enough, this word which in no uncertain
terms demands my loyalty offers me what I need and what I
want in my heart of hearts. It offers me the one thing necessary,
which I can't give to myself or achieve through my exertions. It
gives me the power to accept myself with the brokenness which
touches every level of my existence. It gives me the power to
accept life in all its fragility and death with all its certainty. It
gives me the almost incredible power to find myself in this
acceptance and to experience the freedom to love another and
ultimately to love God, the world, and all that is in it. True
freedom is a gift before it is a power, and the word of address is
marked as personal because it confers upon me the gift of being
free, of being a person, of being a self. This word heals the splits
within. In hearing it, I know I belong, I have a place to stand and
to rest because of this word of another.

In different ways, all of the New Testament and the whole
of Christian tradition are aware that the word Jesus speaks, and
the word Jesus *is,* are not really "words about" the human
situation or simply models to follow. He and his words are
words of address which demand loyalty and confer freedom.[29]
Paul is quite aware that he has not chosen a philosophy or even
a way of life. Rather, he has been *called* to be an apostle, and he
and his fellow Christians make up the group of those called: the
ek-*kle*-sia; the Greek root means "call" or "summon." John's
Jesus says: "You have not chosen me; I have chosen you." From
the very beginning, the message was preached, proclaimed, and
it was recognized that this living word was by no means a
summary of human wisdom.[30] It was nothing less than the

power of God, which demands from us *hypakouen*—not "obedience" as submission to the will of another, but rather an attentive and willing listening, a *hearkening* to this powerful and
personal word. This dependence on the living word of Jesus
insured that when Luther searched desperately for a "merciful
God," he would not be satisfied by truths or propositions. Only
the word of God to and for him in all of his uniqueness would
do—a word which told him that, although a sinner, he was
accepted and that God's unlikely verdict would prevail, because
this and nothing else is what it means to be God.[31]

What all of this means is that Jesus' word as read, reflected
on, preached and lived is effective in many ways which we can
experience and think about. When we do think about it, it is
evident that Jesus' word now, today, still acts in the way that *only
the words of living persons do*. It creates life and it gives us the
freedom to be our real selves as only the genuine personal word
can and does. This word of Jesus is *mediated* today in a variety of
ways—all of them, I believe, rooted in the New Testament as the
living word. But this mediation does not stop it from being his
word. Those who mediated his word wanted it to be his word,
not theirs, and it appears that the only motive they had in
speaking and writing was their loyalty to him. Remarkably, they
gave us at times such a clear outline of his person that the real
Jesus one perceives in their writing stands as a judge and critic
even over some of the things they made him do and say.[32]

1.61   But this mediated word of Jesus shows that it is still really
his word in a definitive way: it bears the stamp of the decisive
event of his life—his death on the cross. As "the word of the
cross" it is his word and not the word that others have placed on
his lips because the cross is diametrically opposed to the word of
human wisdom which we try to speak about God. Human wisdom is not comfortable with the cross and with the God who
participated there in the suffering and brokenness of the world.

The cross is the foolishness of God which is wiser than the wisdom of men and the weakness of God which is stronger than the strength of men. As the word of the cross, Jesus' mediated word, like his death itself, is a judgment[33] upon our unbroken confidence in our ability to save ourselves through our religiosity and our "goodness." But—the paradox again!—this judgment does not condemn us but frees us to be our real selves, before God and with one another. The word of the cross is the word which man does not and cannot speak on his own; it is the word which man always resists. Therefore, when it is spoken, it is evidently not man's word but Jesus' own word.

1.7   The New Testament as the Response to Jesus' Word

Jesus' word was handed on, mediated, in many ways. Sometimes people repeated his words; sometimes they told stories about what he did and about the stories and parables he told; sometimes they made "dogmatic" statements about him, sang hymns, made him a part of their prayers and exhorted others in his name. In all of these ways, they were responding personally to the word of Jesus—both to the word he spoke and to the word which he was. But it is important to note something about these stories, parables, liturgical fragments and exhortations: they are not simply *about* Jesus. They are above all a response to him, to the one who is experienced as *living.*[34] These first witnesses, these earliest followers of Jesus, wrote their Gospels and their letters, celebrated liturgies and instructed converts, not because they were concerned about something which *had happened* a generation or two before their time. For them, what had happened then was of interest only because of what *was happening now*, at the present moment, in their churches and in themselves. All of the words which they seem to be speaking *about* Jesus are really words which they speak in response to the *present* Jesus and to his word which is still being spoken to them as a living, personal word. The word which they speak is for this reason an *extension* or *prolongation* of his word. It is his word as mediated.

Now it is precisely *this* word which is recorded in the New Testament.[35] If we call the word of these first followers of Jesus the *kerygma* or proclamation, then the New Testament is privileged kerygma in which Jesus' own word is handed on. And it is a word which shows by its life-giving power that it is the word of one who lives. It is superficial, inadequate and therefore erroneous to regard the New Testament as a book of stories and statements about Jesus. The New Testament is rather Jesus' own word as heard and preached and lived by a group called to do precisely this—the ek-kle-sia, which is *called* to do nothing else. If the New Testament is called a *book,* then it must be emphasized that it is by no means a mere record of thoughts spoken at another time but is a personal, living word, which, like every living and personal word, is a word of judgment and a word of grace, a word which makes us aware of our sinfulness and estrangement, a word which calls us to authentic existence and empowers us to accept it.

To summarize here: the New Testament as an active text, as preached and heard and lived, is the *event* in which I experience that Jesus is the Christ. It is the event in which the personal, living and transforming word of Jesus of Nazareth at one time becomes his personal, living and transforming word for all time. It is this word which reveals that Jesus lives. To say that the New Testament is an active book in the sense in which the word is used here *is the same thing as to say that Jesus is the Christ.* The task of christology and of all theology is to understand the New Testament as the living and active word of Jesus, who lives, so that his word may continue to be spoken in language which is understood today. Where Jesus' word is spoken and understood, he is present.

1.71 Because the New Testament is Jesus' own word *in* the words of those who spoke under the impact of his words and his person, the problem of the language in which these words are spoken becomes acute. But note: the word "language" here refers not primarily to the vocabulary and grammar of New Testament Greek but rather to the *resources of thought and expression* which were available to those who wanted to give new voice to the word of Jesus they had heard. Because these resources of thought and expression were different from ours, they often spoke in a way which is difficult to understand today. The New Testament speaks of Jesus as *kyrios,* or *soter* or *huios tou anthropou,* and although these words can *in a sense* be translated as *Lord, Savior,* and *Son of Man,* they really don't become intelligible as a result of this "translation." These words can really be decoded and deciphered only if they are heard in their historical context and only if we strive to make a careful judgment about what they are *really* saying as distinct from what they are *apparently* saying. This means that the New Testament can be understood only if it is read historically and critically.[36]

1.72 The words "historical-critical method" or "historical-critical hermeneutic" (that is, method or technique of interpretation) can be understood in different ways. Some theologians understand by these terms simply a way of grasping the meaning of any document, ancient or modern. I do not. As I understand these terms, they are not merely *tools* which, along with others, may be found in the arsenal of the good scriptural theologian. Rather, they are a *form of understanding* which is demanded by the very nature of the New Testament as the living word of Jesus. They refer to this form of understanding which is necessary for theology and which is called for by faith itself. Although a full treatment of the subject is obviously beyond the scope of this book, it will be appropriate to state as briefly as possible the relationship of historical-critical method to theology and to faith.

Historical hermeneutic strives to hear, to hearken to a text by learning to understand the language in which it was written. As noted above, the word "language" here refers to more than the vocabulary of a foreign tongue; it means the vocabulary of a foreign *world*. It refers not simply to morphological and syntactical rules which are at variance with those of our own tongue, but rather, and much more, to the historical and cultural situation of the author, to the imagery which was available to him, to the world-view of his society (which conditioned him whether he accepted it or not). All of these provide a writer with certain possibilities of expression, which are exactly analogous to "language" in the narrower and more usual sense of the word. And all of these factors, which are elements of "language" in the broad sense, are themselves conditioned by history, dependent for their meaning on events and interpretations of the past, and intelligible today only to the extent to which we are aware of those events and interpretations.[37]

Historical-critical hermeneutic, as I understand the term here, strives simply to understand the New Testament by understanding its "language." As a result of this, it is in a position to see that the New Testament is neither biography nor historiography nor nineteenth century apologetic. It sees the New Testament as *kerygma*—as the continuing proclamation of the word which Jesus spoke and of the word which he *was*—as the claim that something which happened *then* is decisive for existence *now*.[38] Because an historical hermeneutic brings to light the resources which the New Testament authors had at their disposal, this method makes it possible to know what the kerygma intended—that is, what is being proclaimed, what the word of Jesus and the word about him is really saying. In recognizing that the cultural situation of the New Testament writers put certain resources of thought and expression at their disposal (and deprived them of others), an historical hermeneutic rejects naive fundamentalism in any form and is free to be radically critical.

Fundamentalism does not interpret the New Testament "according to its literal meaning" (as fundamentalists are fond of asserting). In fact, it does not interpret the New Testament at all; it interprets the *words* into which the New Testament has been translated, and it does so in accordance with the meanings these words have acquired *in other and more recent religious and cultural traditions.* In contrast, an historical hermeneutic is genuinely conservative, in that it interprets the New Testament against its own background and in terms of its own world and does not judge its assertions in terms of cultural contexts which appeared, in some cases, more than a thousand years after the New Testament was written.

An historical hermeneutic is free to be radically critical because it is in a position to distinguish the *manner* and *form* in which an assertion is made from the *content* of the assertion. An historical hermeneutic is, in principle, open to a program of demythologization (a term meaning not the rejection of myth but the *identification* of myth). The word "myth" is understood in a most general sense as "the historically and culturally conditioned imagery which is at the disposal of members of a specific community when they wish to express the meaning of events." The identification of "myth" in this sense is extremely important for the interpretation of the New Testament (and the Old Testament as well) for two reasons: first, when myth is identified, one is free to ask what was actually being asserted by means of the myth; second, one is free to accept the Christian message without being forced to adopt the imagery and world-view of first century Jewish and Hellenistic thought. The gain in intellectual honesty is enormous.

The historical hermeneutic which is being described here is also *critical:* it strives to discover criteria on the basis of which one can make intelligent judgments about what Scripture is actually asserting and about what the challenge of faith actually is. Intelligent judgments of this type are not repugnant to the kerygma, to the proclamation of Jesus; they are rather *demanded* by it. This proclamation makes demands on human beings who are human because they are capable of intelligent and free response. We respond to the kerygma with intelligence and freedom, not by sacrificing or mortifying our intelligence, but by striving to make an intelligent judgment about what the proclamation *intends*.[39] But only a critical questioning of the kerygma can show what this is. Such critical questioning does not spring from an inclination to doubt the truth of Scripture; it does not demand evidence for the *truth* of what Scripture is asserting. It rather examines the evidence to determine as carefully as possible *what* the New Testament is asserting. A critical hermeneutic does not force faith to submit itself to reason, but it does recognize that faith is offered to rational beings who must rely on their intelligence to find out what faith really demands.

In view of this, it is most unfortunate that historical-critical hermeneutic often has to defend itself against the charge of competing with faith as a source of knowledge about God, or, even worse, of undermining faith. Therefore it is important to note that a critical hermeneutic of the New Testament serves faith by attempting to discover exactly what faith is called on to believe.

The historical-critical interpretation of the New Testament is a specifically modern achievement, and it has frequently called into question many things which Christians believed or at least asserted in the name of faith.[40] For this reason, this method of interpretation is often charged with hostility to faith and with conspiracy to destroy its foundations. But this charge is based on a misunderstanding, both of critical hermeneutic and of faith. Faith is an act of knowing. It is therefore an appropriation of meaning and one which human intelligence seeks from the depths of its being. Both the call to faith and faith's own expression of what it has found are mediated through the structures of human reason.[41]

Faith is therefore not alien to reason. It does not dwell in a sphere of its own, above and beyond the mundane concerns of human intelligence, nor is it called upon to preserve its purity by offering reason coexistence without cohabitation. In faith the inner dynamisms of reason are fulfilled. Reason is made for faith, and when it asks what the Christian proclamation really intends, it is not trespassing on sacred ground, but rather judging the evidence on the basis of its own "made for faith" structure, its most basic structural a priori, without which it could not even function as reason.[42]

Faith does not have to defend itself against historical-critical interpretation of the New Testament. Real faith calls for such a hermeneutic precisely because it takes seriously the Jesus whom it has encountered in the Church, in word and in sacrament. To say that faith must be critical is simply to assert that faith is an act of understanding which must be made responsibly. To demand that the critical interpretation of which faith avails itself should also be historical is simply to point out that responsible understanding of the spoken and written word is possible only for one who understands the language in which this word is spoken or written (again, in the broad sense of the word "language"—that is, the various resources in thought and imagery which were available to those who wrote and spoke in New Testament times).

1.8 The Crisis of Christology

Only when we have understood Jesus' word, as mediated by the New Testament, can that word be effective in our lives, transforming them and leading to faith. And only when this has happened can we begin the other very difficult task of speaking this word in language which is understood today. The problem today (although it is by no means a new problem) is that in all of the churches there is so much talk about Jesus which is devoid of real content and is simply empty, pietistic jargon. Such talk is a perversion, but it caters so effectively to our desire to escape from both the real God and the real Jesus that it is hardly likely to disappear on its own. Such talk, of course, is without power to heal our brokenness and to create new life within us, and many in our day are denied this experience of healing and of new life because they confuse the prevalent babble about Jesus with Jesus himself.

1.81 In principle the solution seems simple: learn to read the New Testament in such a way that the real Jesus Christ can be found there; find in the New Testament not a collection of stories about Jesus but rather Jesus himself, mediated through the impact he had on those who believed in him. When this real Jesus is found, then we can interpret our whole existence, all of the real possibilities implied in the task of living and dying, in terms of him, his challenge and his offer.

In essence this *is* the right solution, but certain factors make it very difficult to act this way "in good conscience." The New Testament is not simply a book written long ago which is discovered by an individual today, who reads it and becomes a believer. The New Testament has a peculiar relationship to the group called by Jesus at the beginning and to the group which has been called in each generation—that is, the *Church.* The New Testament did not come into being because individuals who had met Jesus "in the flesh" felt impelled to record their individual experiences of him.[43] (It is quite probable that nothing in the New Testament was written by anyone who had actually known Jesus before his death.)[44] The New Testament was written by those who had encountered Jesus in the liturgy, the preaching, the prayer, the faith, the life of the *Church.* The New Testament is above all a record of the faith of the Church, and because this faith was a response to the living Lord, the New Testament has the power of mediating him and making his call present to all generations. Each of us can read the New Testament today and reflect on ways of reading it rightly only because it has been handed on through the years and placed in our hands by the group called to do just this—to insure that Jesus and his word remain the living word of address and never become a sterile and lifeless word about things which happened long ago.[45] The New Testament is the book of the Church because it came to be in the Church to fulfill the needs of the Church and it has continued to do this up to the present moment. The New Testament is the expression of the faith of the Church of (mainly) the second and third generation, and it has created the faith of the Church of succeeding generations. As is obvious from this, the New Testament and the Church are not separable entities which could be put in a contrasting or competitive relationship. The definition of one is included in the definition of the other; it is quite accurate to call the New Testament the book written in, by and for the Church and to call the Church the community of those who hearken to the New Testament word.[46]

But it is precisely this which causes the difficulty. The Church (and the term here includes all of the Churches which call themselves Christian) expresses its faith in Jesus in words which are not simply those of the New Testament but which reflect events in Church life during the almost two thousand year period since the death of Jesus of Nazareth. These events themselves are very diverse: disagreements and attempts to mediate between the struggling parties, meetings of the leadership of the Church which attempted to find ways of speaking that could express the ancient faith in terms appropriate to new questions and problems. At many times the disputes were more personal or political than theological, and often enough questions were raised to which no answer could be found, simply because the questions themselves were posed in the wrong way or were based on false or doubtful assumptions.

As a result, after almost two millennia of Church life and history, the Churches today express their faith in Jesus Christ largely in a terminology derived from the official decisions of several of the early councils (meetings of the bishops of predominantly the Eastern or Greek Church), which took place between the years 325 and 687 A.D. Now this language, this terminology, is by no means the empty and pietistic jargon alluded to above. It has on countless occasions served the faith of the Church and of the individual Christian. But one thing must be admitted: the ecumenical councils of the three and one half century period mentioned and the Church's statement of its faith in Jesus Christ which is derived from them do give us a Jesus who seems significantly different from the one we encounter in a genuinely historical and critical reading of the New Testament, particularly of the Synoptic Gospels.[47]

Briefly, the differences could be summarized in this way. In varying degrees, Mark, Matthew and Luke present Jesus as a very human being who in various stages or at different times enters the divine sphere and now lives there definitively ("at the right hand of God"). This had certainly happened by the resurrection, but it was already true in a hidden way during Jesus' public life. In Mark the theme of the misunderstanding of the disciples shows that even though the veil is sometimes lifted (in the miracle and exorcism stories) the hiddenness remains.[48] For Matthew and Luke, Jesus belongs (still as a human being) more clearly to the divine sphere, even during his public life; the theophany, the public manifestation of God at the time of Jesus' baptism, gives good evidence of this.[49] In addition, both Matthew and Luke push the presence of Jesus in the divine sphere back to his infancy and beyond. John's Jesus has been in the divine realm from the beginning—that is, from eternity. Paul, strangely enough, seems to be at home both with the Jesus whom God made Lord and Christ at the resurrection *and* with the Christ who pre-existed his manifestation in human form.[50] The ecumenical councils are very selective and clearly rest their case on John and on those elements in Paul which assert or presuppose the pre-existence of Christ. For all of the councils, Jesus Christ is, in his *person,* a divine being who entered the world, lived, died and then returned to the divine sphere where he had lived before the beginning of the world.[51]

The crisis of Christology in modern times has come about because of the tension between the Christ of the councils and the Jesus of the Synoptic tradition. It can, of course, be argued that in the Synoptic tradition as a whole there is ample evidence for every statement ever made by a council about Jesus Christ. But a closer examination of the same Synoptic tradition showed that it was far from uniform and that Matthew and Luke, though very different from each other, give us a Jesus who is far more "conciliar" than the man from Nazareth presented by Mark. The very diversity of the pictures of Jesus given in the Synoptic tradition (in which the earlier strata give us a more human and vulnerable Jesus) made a further question inevitable: Who was Jesus really? As time passed, had his story been rewritten on the basis of hopes and dreams that had little to do with the real man who lived and died? This question led nineteenth century Protestant theology on a search for the historical Jesus which has been fateful for Protestant thought for over a century and a half, and there is every evidence that serious Catholic theology has begun to face the same problem in the last third of the twentieth century. We will discuss the problems posed and the possibilities opened up by the various "quests of the historical Jesus" in a later chapter, but here one point should be made. The search for the real Jesus before the councils and before the Gospels has almost never been motivated by lack of faith or by the desire to prove the Christ irrelevant to life in the real world. The search for the real, "historical" Jesus has been motivated by a deeply Christian insight—the insight that, although Jesus as the *Christ* is the object of our faith, this Christ is the one who defined himself in a determinate human existence. As we noted at the beginning of this chapter, to say "Jesus Christ" is not to utter a name; it is to make a confession of faith. Faith in the Christ is meaningless unless *Jesus* is the Christ. What happened *then* is of absolute importance, because Christian faith asserts that in Jesus God has become definitively involved in history, forever touched by the times and places in which Jesus lived and through them touching every time and place up to the end of the world. The Christ in whom we believe remains *this* human being, with this unique and unrepeatable past, and if he is alive now, he lives in continuity with this past. Even more to the point, the fact that he lives now makes it necessary to use such words as "past" and "then" only in a paradoxical sense. Because he lives, his past is part of his present—and ours. Faith asserts that God put his seal of approval on this life and this death in such a way that *this human history* is God's history and therefore it is here that we are to look for that foolishness of God which is wiser than the wisdom of men.[52] We are called to believe not despite or apart from this human history which is God's own, but through it and by it. And we are no more dispensed from the ordinary human ways of making contact with the personal history of Jesus than his contemporaries were dispensed from using their eyes and ears to come to know the man who was God's Word to them. The divine in Jesus does not compete with the human.[53] To say that the Word became flesh means nothing unless the historical person, Jesus of Nazareth, is the one who makes God real, makes God happen, precisely in his spatial, temporal and material uniqueness. Anything else may be good Platonism but it is bad theology.

Put simply, the crisis in Christology has come about because of one question: "Is Jesus of Nazareth really the same person as the Christ of the councils, the Christ of traditional faith?" The crisis created by this question shook Protestant theology in the nineteenth century, but it is even more serious for Catholic theology today, and this was inevitable. The "protest" in the word "Protestant" was largely against beliefs and practices which lacked a demonstrable scriptural pedigree. Catholics, on the other hand, rejected many Protestant positions on the basis of "tradition"—norms of belief and practice which had been handed down in the Church and had gone unquestioned, often for centuries. These traditions were often—almost always in significant matters—*interpretations* of Scripture, but they were frequently interpretations which were by no means self-evident, and in demanding their acceptance as a condition of faith, Popes, bishops and Catholic theologians rested their case not on Scripture alone but on Scripture as authoritatively interpreted by the teaching Chuch.[54]

Catholicism defined itself against the Reformation through the work of a council—that of Trent—and the authority of the ecumenical councils (by definition, meetings of bishops which were later approved by the Pope) has grown during the past four centuries, and especially during the last century. Increasingly, the theology taught in the theological seminaries in Rome came to treat the councils (and the creeds which they produced) as the real or primary sources of theology and has tended to read scripture "through conciliar glasses." This *de facto* tendency was given *de jure* status in Pius XII's 1950 encyclical *Humani Generis,* where it was affirmed that it is the task of the theologian to show that the content or meaning of those statements authoritatively taught by the Church is already contained in Scripture and that its meaning is unchanged.[55]

Protestants themselves, although not fond of the tradition principle, took the dogmatic formulas of the early councils (325 to 687) quite seriously until well into the nineteenth century (and those Churches which have attempted to immunize or isolate themselves from history still do). But in the past century Protestant theology has increasingly turned away from the "Christ of dogma"—a construction which they feel has little to do with the man from Nazareth—and many have written off the conciliar period as offering little more than the Hellenization of the Gospel. They have been joined in recent years by many Catholics who can find no fault with the historical studies which lead to this conclusion (although the term "Hellenization of the Gospel" seems rather quaint today and has dropped out of use).[56]

In the course of this book I will suggest that traditional Catholic attitudes on the one hand and some modern Protestant and recent Catholic attitudes on the other have been somewhat one-sided. Scripture (above all the New Testament) and the councils can both be thought of as events of Church life, but they belong on different levels and should not be forced to play the same role. If this is seen, both have a role to play in answering the question: "Who is Jesus Christ?" For reasons implied above, it is beyond doubt that the New Testament must be given absolute priority as a *source* of Christology, the reflection about Jesus Christ. As a word of power, the Gospel or good news is the evidence that Jesus is the Christ, and in terms of its content it defines the Christ in the historical reality of Jesus of Nazareth. If the councils are ever accorded *this* kind of priority, then Scripture cannot be read as intended and it has lost its proper position as the norm of Christian faith and life which is binding on the Church itself (and the Church's own identity would be in danger).[57] However, the decisions of the councils on matters of faith represent the reflection of the listening and teaching Church, to which the Spirit has been promised.[58] This Church is made up of those with whom the Lord himself will be until the end of the world, and to strip the councils of any effective role in Christian faith is to call into question the presence of the living Lord in his Church.

A qualitative difference between Scripture and the councils *as sources* must be maintained. Doing this is one of the major tasks of this book, and in preliminary form this is the solution I propose.

In the strict sense of the word "source," *Scripture,* as preached, heard and lived in the community of those who follow Jesus Christ, is the only *source* of theology. However, if the scriptural message is to be understood and not merely parroted, it must be articulated in the language of each successive generation, despite all of the dangers attendant on such a process. For this reason, and precisely because of its concern for the purity and integrity of the scriptural message, it is appropriate for the Church to establish *parameters* within which this articulation must proceed, *boundaries* beyond which a legitimate solution cannot be sought. These parameters and boundaries take account of the thought and culture, the philosophy and world-view of a given age, and to this degree they are conditioned by the time and place and world-view of those who use them. Their truth consists in their ability to safeguard the Christian message within a given historical context. They are and will remain true in respect to the historical context in which they came to be, but if the *words* in which they are phrased come to have different meanings in the course of time, the original sense of the conciliar formulas (these parameters and boundaries) can be distorted or even lost.[59] Just as we recognize the existence of the literary forms in Scripture (broadly speaking: ways of thinking and speaking which are alien to us today), so also we have to recognize the existence of literary forms in conciliar documents. Otherwise we run the risk of forcing the councils and their creeds to deal with problems which those who framed them could not have foreseen. Even worse, we would try to force ourselves to accept the philosophy and world-view of Greek Christians of sixteen hundred years ago as the price of faith in Jesus Christ today. But such a mortification of the intellect is neither human nor good, and therefore it cannot be Christian.

The implication of all of this is that the crisis of Christology has come about because the councils have been used as the primary sources of theology and that the Churches, basing themselves on these conciliar formulas and creeds, have for many years been saying things which are formally quite true (within the framework of the language in which they were first uttered) but which by now have become almost totally unintelligible to present day Christians and to those with whom these latter would like to share their faith. It is also implied that this is a particularly serious problem for Catholics because of the Catholic tendency, born of the post-Reformation polemic, to give to the councils pride of place in determining the faith of the Church and the individual believer. A final important point has not been implied and will be stated here: because of its sense of continuity, because of its awareness that Scripture *is* Scripture only when it is preached, heard and lived in the *Church,* Catholic thought has an extremely important contribution to make in regard to the positive assessment of the achievements of the early councils and in regard to determining how that achievement may be repeated today and in the future in worlds totally different from the Greco-Roman Christian world of the fourth to seventh centuries.

In the next chapter we will turn to the story of the early councils and of the christological controversies which brought them into being and which, in their own way, they resolved. I believe that this step is important, not because the obligatory chapter on the development of theology during the patristic period has become a hallowed part of all Christology courses or even because the Fathers of the Church provided ways of thinking and speaking about Jesus Christ which must determine our own thought and speech today. We will examine the development of christological thought from New Testament times to the seventh century because this period has been fateful for all subsequent thought about Jesus Christ. On the surface, the influence of this period has usually been positive and benign; beneath the surface its influence has been more questionable. I believe that the time has come for Catholic theology to achieve freedom in respect to this conciliar, patristic tradition and to do this in the name of the absolute priority of the New Testament as a source of faith and life. But freedom *from* the councils is desirable only in this very limited sense—only if it means the refusal to treat the councils as a source of faith and of theology. In the proper sense of the word "source," this belongs to Scripture alone.

I believe, however, that achieving freedom from the councils in this limited sense means at the same time becoming free *for* the councils in a broad and important sense. Councils have been essential to Church life from Nicaea to Vatican II not because of their positive doctrine but because of the linguistic conventions they established—ways of speaking which did not in themselves distort the faith and which provided a solid basis for further reflection as faith strove to deepen itself. These linguistic conventions imply that certain ways of speaking are true to the Jesus of the New Testament and other ways of speaking are not.[60] Their concern is to keep the real Jesus unchanged, to prevent the alteration or dissolution of his image by any of the popular or learned philosophies of the day.[61] They do this, as they must, in making use of the language and conceptuality of precisely these popular and learned philosophies, and the formulas which they have left us make sense only in terms of this same language and conceptuality. But within this framework they are of enduring importance for both theology and faith because the dangers they saw are perennial; human thought in every age will always try to domesticate Jesus.

However, the councils are important, too, for what they did not achieve—for their failure to break free of the immobile God which was the legacy of the Greek world and to do this in the name of the living God who was their birthright. The positive achievements of the early councils can be found in the answers they gave to questions which arose in a world very different from that of the New Testament. The negative effects of these same councils are due to their failure to question the legitimacy of at least some of these questions.

The Christian Message
and the Greek World

2.1 Introduction

Even before the writing of the Gospels, Christianity had
begun to leave the Jewish world of its childhood and to address
and engage that world which called itself "Greek." The term
had lost many of its national and ethnic connotations. It was no
longer the world of classical Greece (and we call it "Hellenistic"
to mark that fact), but it was Greek in language, and its philosophy, although eclectic, was very much the heir of classical Greek
thought. The Church which began to engage this world from
about the middle of the first century was not yet fully formed or
secure in its own identity. The New Testament itself is the
convincing evidence that it was in this encounter that the
Church discovered its true identity,[62] for the place taken by
Paul's writings, his "Gospel," would otherwise be totally unintelligible.[63] Paul had been preaching the Gospel to the "Greeks"
for years before the writing of the Gospel of Mark, and he
himself had been initiated into the faith in a community—that of
Damascus—which had strong Gentile and international lean-
ings.

The early Church came into being and found its identity
largely through the preaching of Paul, with its emphasis on
God's absolutely unmerited acceptance and on Christ as the end
of the law. There is no doubt that Paul was responsible for a
radical and definitive change in the early Church, but he added
nothing alien or foreign. The inner dynamic of the message of

35

Jesus made it inevitable that Christianity would cease to be simply a Jewish sect and would become a faith with world-embracing claims,[64] and the fall of Jerusalem in the year 70 A.D. sealed the fate of Jewish Christianity and turned the face of the new faith definitively toward the Hellenistic, Gentile world. Certain effects of this turn are of interest to us now.

2.2   The Character and Tendencies of Greek Thought

Although most of the New Testament was written by men not unaffected by the popular philosophy of the age (since they wrote in Greek this was inevitable), most of those who wrote it shared an historical and dynamic view of reality. They had been formed directly and indirectly by the Jewish vision of /a God whose divinity was manifest in the fact that he was Lord of history. These were men whose God was active in the world. This was a God who rejoiced with those he had made and shared their sorrow, who might repent of what he had done and assume a totally new stance toward those whose God he had chosen to be. The men who wrote the New Testament were not concerned with essences, stable qualities or changeless natures of either God or the world. In regard to both, they were interested in how God and man had *acted,* what they had *done.* They were intrigued less by ideas than by events. Instead of theorizing about the attributes of God they recited stories about his definitive entry into history. Their God was not pure being but one who had led his chosen ones out of the land of Egypt and out of the house of bondage and who was therefore a God of hope, a God for the future.[65]

Such ways of thinking were alien to the Hellenistic world to which the Church turned increasingly as the first century drew to a close, and this made it hard for that world to understand what the New Testament was really asserting, despite the fact that it was written in Greek.[66] In time this would lead to false interpretation and to profound misunderstanding, as the new faith left its Jewish roots behind and left the text of the New Testament without an historical context. (It is interesting to note that the first example of this development antedates the writing of the Gospels; in Corinth Paul encountered the resistance of the Greek mind to his theology of the cross and he criticized the resulting "resurrection theology" as a fundamental distortion of the central truth of faith.)[67] It is precisely the uniqueness of the New Testament as a source of faith and theology which makes it necessary to understand something of the Greek world and its patterns of thought.

Greek thought developed for over a thousand years, and many of its more profiled protagonists were irreconcilably opposed to one another—a fact which obviously makes it difficult to find much evidence of continuity in doctrine. But beneath the differences there are certain underlying *tendencies* or *directions* which are constant, at least from the time of Parmenides (born in 515 B.C.) and to the end of the the period which interests us here (about the end of the seventh century A.D.).[68] When I speak of the Greek mind, it is to this period and to these tendencies that I am referring.

2.21 One of these tendencies belongs in first place here because it is probably at the root of all of the others; for Greek thought, to *be* in the fullest and deepest sense means to be stable, constant, enduring, and ultimately to be *immutable,* without change. Change implies imperfection, a deficiency in being, a failure to be fully real. The Greek mind seeks that which underlies change and remains constant—that which is immune to change and untouched by it. And as a result the Greek mind will never be sympathetic to the new, the unexpected, the unheard of, and will have little understanding for the God "who makes all things new."

Note carefully: the problem does not lie with the dedication of Greek thinkers to the stable and the enduring—this can be paralleled in some of the most profound passages in the Old Testament[69]—but rather their conviction that the power to act in a new and heretofore unheard of way belies imperfection. The roots of this conviction can certainly be found in the fragments of the Ionian philosophers of nature of the sixth and fifth centuries before Christ, and it reached finished form in Aristotle's assertion that change is possible only in a being whose reality is tempered by the admixture of purely potential being—in the final analysis, of *that which is not.* For such a philosophy, a God who is at once eternal and living will be too great a challenge.

This esteem for the changeless casts a deep shadow over the Greek view of time and place and the material things which have their existence there. For Plato, the really real is the immaterial, the spiritual, the ideal, and life in the world is a fall from these heights; it is essentially an imprisoned existence.[70] For Aristotle, motion itself is a sign that the merely potential plays a dominant role in the existence of a material thing. For both of these philosophers—two of the finest minds in the history of Greek thought and therefore unparalleled in their influence—matter, time and space, and the changing events in which the unique individual works out his destiny there, have only a limited, diminished and partial reality. Unfortunately this view had effects which could not be confined to the world of matter and to the Greek inability to take it seriously (although it is interesting to speculate on what a mind like Aristotle's might have achieved within a tradition capable of taking the experimental method seriously). Greek fascination with the universal idea, the ideal form, made it difficult to deal with the human individual, the free person, and the philosophies derived from Greece have been significantly weak in this respect.[71]

2.22 A second tendency or group of tendencies in Greek thought is a direct result of this inability to deal with the human person; even in its Christian form, the Greek mind was never at home with the concept or fact of *freedom*. Freedom was always defined as indifference or indeterminacy—a situation which seems to imply a lack of or failure in being—and as a result it was extremely difficult to see in freedom a perfection, a value. The thesis of classical Thomism that God's self-love is not free but rather necessary, because fully determined by its object, indicates that, for this philosophy and all those derived from it, freedom, even when defined with the greatest care, cannot be an unconditioned or transcendental value.[72] This lack of esteem for human freedom will later have very negative effects when Christian thought tries to find a positive role for the humanity of Jesus Christ.

There is another closely allied tendency within this second group—another form taken by the Greek world's antipathy to the experiential and unique. This world would live to the end of its days under the spell of Plato, and in its eyes the unique historical event could not be of ultimate meaning. The words of Chrysippus are typical, and they echo the pathos and pessimism of all ancient civilization when they recount the myth of the eternal return: "Socrates and Plato will live again and every man with his friends and fellow citizens. Every village, every town and every field will appear again, and this not only once but time without end." The Greeks could be quite interested in the past—Thucydides, Herodotus and Polybius bear witness to this—but for them history remained the field where man, as a spectator, might discern eternal laws of conduct and political action. It was not the domain where man himself might change and where his own reality was at stake.

Christianity itself constitutes an insoluble problem for this Greek view of history, because Christianity is an historical faith.

To assert this is to assert much more than the fact that Christianity appeared on the stage of world history at a certain time and under concrete historical conditions; this would be true of every religion and every philosophy. To call Christianity an historical faith is to assert that God manifested himself once and for all in the unique historical event we know as Jesus Christ. This Jesus is not simply the teacher of a new way of righteousness or the bearer of a new doctrine, but is, in his unique historical individuality, God's Word to human beings in all centuries from the first through the twentieth to the end of time. To call Christianity an historical faith means that the event which stands at the beginning, remains permanently valid. God spoke there and then and Christian faith is the believing reception of something which *happened* and therefore is still happening. To call Christianity an historical faith is to affirm that Christianity can never be "dehistoricized," dissolved into a set of statements or doctrines above time and independent of history. It is the very *historicity* of Jesus—he transcended history by being involved in it and subject to it—which makes it so very difficult for Greek thought to cope with him. Faced with the New Testament evidence, the Greek mind will affirm the historical dimension of Jesus—that is, his humanity—as a *fact,* but it will always be at a loss in finding something for that humanity to do, and in attributing to it a real role in the saving of the human race.[73]

2.23 A third group of tendencies in Greek thought can be identified—tendencies which have to do with the nature of God and our knowledge of him. The Greek *Theos* was separated from the world by an unbridgeable chasm. He is the unmoved mover, beyond being and non-being. His unity is absolute and he must be preserved from all contact with and contamination by the multiplicity and diversity of the world. God is alone in his heaven and man is the measure of all things on earth. Note again: the problem is not that Greek thought affirmed the *transcendence* of God—this is an essential element of biblical faith, and in the most anthropomorphic texts of the Old Testament, God remains the one "on whose face no man can look and live."[74] The problem is rather that the transcendence of God is interpreted as *remoteness,* and for this reason it is impossible for God to be both transcendent and immanent, heavenly and worldly, totally other and totally engaged.

2.24 Closely allied to this banishing of God from the world of life and action is the final tendency to be mentioned here: the inability of Greek thought to deal with paradox, the apparent contradiction, and to see life as the "coincidence of opposites." "Moderation in all things" remained the Greek ideal, and conflicts were resolved by finding a golden mean. For such a system of thought, a God who shows his power in freely accepting the sinner into his company is too engaged, and the sinful human being whom he accepts is too ignoble to remain the measure of all things. For such a system of thought, a God who takes the brokenness of the world to himself is nonsense and a man who must come to the end of his ways before the ways of God begin is both an affront and an insult. It is here that the inability of the Greek mind to deal with paradox had its most damaging consequences: this world could neither comprehend nor welcome the central themes of Pauline thought—neither the theme of God's gratuitous justification of the sinner nor the theme of God's revelation of his power and wisdom in the weakness and foolishness of the cross.[75] It is significant that these themes disappear from the Pauline Churches soon after Paul's own time (their absence from the Deutero-Pauline literature is striking) and that the specifically Pauline paradoxes of the cross, of faith, and of justification are absent from the entire Greek patristic tradition. The moments at which these Pauline themes have surfaced coincide with those periods in which historical and cultural

factors have turned men away from the Greek way and toward
the God who participated in the weakness and brokenness of the
human situation on a certain day and in a certain place.

Perhaps the term "Hellenization of the Gospel" is not as
quaint and dated as it appeared to be. But if we use it today, it
will be wise to see it not as a danger for Christian thought
during the first seven centuries but rather as a perennial threat.
The Greek way is seductive and its leading exponents through
the centuries have been brilliant and persuasive. Too often in
the past the attempt was made to combat it with weapons at
once unworthy and inadequate—anti-intellectualism and a human foolishness which has nothing to do with the foolishness of
God (which is wiser than the *wisdom* of men). Christian faith
would be well served by an analysis of Greek thought which
would lay bare the roots of its hostility to freedom, to history
and to life, and its consequent inabiilty to cope with the free
person who stands before the living God and who can find that
peace which the world cannot give in the midst of the brokenness of the world. These few pages here cannot claim complete-
ness, even as a summary. They merely intend to suggest how
deep are the problems, how pervasive the dangers, for any
theology which would allow the writings of the Greek patristic
period (even the councils and their creeds) to usurp the role of
the New Testament as the source of Christian faith and life.

2.3   Christology from the New Testament to Nicaea

Christology does not begin with the New Testament, even
for us. A careful reading of even the earliest writings of the New
Testament shows that within twenty years of the death of Jesus,
reflection on and speculation about his life and death and continuing influence had already reached an advanced stage.[76] Obviously, such reflection began at that moment when a man or
woman who had met Jesus began to ask who he was and how he

was related to the one whom the Old Testament usually called "the Lord." It is for this reason that the New Testament itself can never be an *absolute* beginning of our thought about Jesus Christ. It is legitimate to ask about the Gospel which was preached before any of the Gospels were written, but it is more than that—it is both inevitable and necessary. The attempt to find the preaching that antedated the Gospels and to trace that development which came to an end in four very different ways in the four Gospels as we have them (the search often called "form criticism"—certainly the most inept and misleading translation in the whole vocabulary of modern theology) is a search *demanded* by the Gospels themselves. The further question of the relationship of the earliest preaching to Jesus of Nazareth himself— that is, the problem of the historical Jesus as it has been envisaged since the middle of this century—is even more urgently demanded by the Gospels and by the whole New Testament, for reasons summarized above in the section on historical-critical method.[77]

It is important to emphasize this fact: it is *the Gospels themselves* which demand that we go behind them; this is not a demand which originates with skeptical modern scholarship. If concern for the historical, for the unique events of Jesus' life were a purely modern phenomenon, then it would be impossible to defend it as an essential category of Christian thought and existence. But this is not the case. The concern for the historical, for the unique past event, is at least as old as the earliest Gospel, that of Mark, which was probably written shortly after 65 A.D. It has become a commonplace of New Testament scholarship that the Gospels are not historical documents in the modern sense of the word, and this is quite true. They were not written by neutral observers but by those who believed firmly that Jesus who died had been raised from the dead and would live forevermore. The Gospels show almost no evidence of biographical interest and they give us little information which is of use in ordering the events of the life of Jesus. But the fact remains: from about the year 67 and for the rest of the century, the Christian community felt the need to ground its preaching in the unique events of the life and death of Jesus of Nazareth.[78] The Gospel writers *intended* to tie their message to events of the past—to events which had happened in definite places and at definite times. They assert that through these events they had received a new understanding of themselves and they cannot separate this new understanding from these events. We are, of course, entitled to ask what knowledge they had of these events which they recount, but the more interesting and fundamental question is always this: What are the events which *really* interest these writers and how can these real interests be distinguished from their merely apparent interests (the ones which always receive great emphasis when the texts are "interpreted literally")? It would be foolish to ignore the nineteen centuries in the history of human thought which have passed since the Gospels were written and to attribute specifically modern historical interest and competence to the evangelists, but it would be a source of great misunderstanding to ignore the concern for the unique historical event called "Jesus of Nazareth" which appears on every page of the Gospels of Matthew, Mark, Luke and John.

However, much of what the New Testament demands for the understanding and preservation of its message has come to be seen many years and even centuries after the close of the New Testament period. In fact, the problem we are facing in this chapter is that of the long delay in fulfilling this demand of the New Testament text itself—a problem occasioned by the alien terrain into which the New Testament moved before the end of the first century. In order to see this problem more clearly and to see the outline of a solution, it will be useful to examine the way the New Testament itself reflected upon and speculated about Jesus Christ and then to examine the development of this reflection in the decades and centuries which followed.

2.31 All of the major writings of the New Testament are concerned more or less explicitly with the relationship of Jesus to the one whom he and they call "God" or "(the) Father." God is clearly "other" than Jesus, and no text of the New Testament identifies Jesus with God.[79] God is always the one to whom Jesus speaks and whose word he hears, and the New Testament never suggests that this dialogue takes place *within* Jesus.[80] It would be alien to the spirit of the New Testament writings to suppose that this dialogue with God is mere pretense or a bit of clever play acting to impress the audience.

But at the same time, Jesus does not speak to this God, hear his word and act in his presence as other human beings do. This Jesus who is a human being and who speaks to God as "someone else" has a unique relationship to God. In a way not easily definable, his dialogue with God is something natural to him. He lives in the presence of God as one who *belongs there.* He never tries to profit from this relationship and he seems to be indifferent to titles and recognition, but this fact simply highlights his calm assurance of being with God at all times, his conviction that he speaks God's word and implicates God in every situation he enters. (In this he is totally unlike the prophets, who resisted the breaking in of God into their lives and who, although they were aware of speaking God's word, spoke it as something foreign and alien which had been imposed on them.[81]) In various ways, all four Gospels (as well as the writings of Paul) not only raise the question of the relationship of Jesus with God; they begin to answer it by suggesting that there is a complexity or even a multiplicity in God as well as in Jesus and that in virtue of this multiplicity there is a common domain where life is shared by God and by Jesus.

The New Testament is tentative here. Matthew, Mark and Luke have not yet developed a *terminology* to deal with the mystery of Jesus (although this does not rule out a profound and advanced implicit Christology in Mark). On the other hand, for both John and Paul the term "Son" is clearly an attempt to speak of Jesus in a way which brings him within the divine life itself.[82] As the New Testament period drew to a close (and long after the major writings of the New Testament were completed)[83] Christian thought about Jesus emphasized more and more his transcendence of the world and his unique relationship with God. As a result, during the second and third centuries a need will be felt to find or fashion a "space" or "place" for Jesus within the very life of God. As this need is met, the problem of multiplicity in God becomes more acute, above all for Greek thought: God is the mysterious, incomprehensible, immutable one, but he has revealed *himself* in Jesus Christ. Jesus is the revelation of *God* and yet he speaks to God as *Father*. The later speculation on the Trinity is an attempt to allow multiplicity and diversity into the divine life without destroying the unity of God.

But this attempt to make a place for Jesus within the life of God causes other difficulties as well, because Jesus is clearly human, above all in the earliest strata of the Synoptic tradition. Can he belong to the divine sphere while remaining one of us? What does this mean for his own inner unity? Is he human *and* divine or must we make a choice? The problem of unity and diversity both within the life of God and within Jesus himself will demand the attention of the Church for the first seven centuries of its existence and is the subject of the great christological and trinitarian councils and creeds. And although the questions and answers were often typically Greek in their terminology and belie a world-view quite alien to that of the New Testament, the problem with which they were trying to cope is a fundamental one—for the New Testament, for the conciliar period and for us.

2.32 Jewish Christianity after the fall of Jerusalem apparently solved the problem by removing Jesus from the divine sphere in the name of the unity of God.[84] Jesus is the good man, the servant, and, in the Old Testament sense, the Son of God, but the stern logic of the Deuteronomic "The Lord our God is one God" made it difficult for the Christian Jew to deal conceptually with the mystery of Jesus. By the end of the first century the future of Christianity clearly lay with the Hellenistic world (to which the Jewish-Christian congregations of the diaspora belonged in any case), and the conservative Jewish Christianity of Palestine continued only in small, heretical groups in which the Christian message was increasingly diluted with Gnostic and apocalyptic speculation.

The Hellenistic world—the "Greeks" to whom the Gospel is now preached—these do not have the same problem with the unity of God as did the Jews. It is not that the Greeks were naive polytheists; at least the educated elite from among whom the Christian apologists and scholars would be drawn certainly were not, and even on the popular level there is good evidence that one high god, transcendent and remote, presided over the multitude of serviceable deities who flitted about the pantheon. But the Hellenistic world had another resource at its disposal. Platonic thought in the fourth century B.C. had so emphasized the unity and immutability of God that any contact between God and world seemed impossible. God could hardly be called Creator, and less than a generation later Aristotle drew the logical conclusion that God did not even know the world.[85]

However, a god who is a mere postulate, needed to guarantee the consistency and cogency of human thought,[86] had no future in a world as yet unprepared to follow this postulate through to its logical conclusion: absolute atheism. The attempt to isolate God from the world never had a chance with the popular mind, and in the centuries that separate the death of Plato from the Christian era, Greek speculative thought turned more and more to the task of building a bridge between the remote "One," divine and absolute, severed from the world of thought and action, and the created world of diversity and change. In the process, the Greek mind continues to think of its austere "god" and of the world as *beings, things,* which simply are "there," endowed with qualities irreconcilably opposed. If, for some reason, these "things" are to be brought together, then a third "thing" must be found which participates in some way in the qualities of each. Gradually, beginning about a century before the Christian era, Greek thought developed the idea of a supreme being, absolutely transcendent in itself, which *manifests, expresses* or *reveals* itself as it moves in a series of steps from unity to diversity. This development reached its conclusion in the work of Plotinus (ca. 205 to 270 A.D.), who argued that the created world is the result of a series of emanations from the divine substance—emanations which are essentially diminished and limited *replicas* of the divine substance which come into being of themselves in the confrontation of the "One" with matter, the principle of diversity and change.[87]

But long before Plotinus, Greek thought had settled on the notion of an *intermediate being* to solve the problem of the separation of the transcendent "One" from the world—a world which could not have come into being without it.[88] Since before the Christian era, this intermediate being had been called *Logos*—the mind, the reason, the thought, the word of the divinity, the "One." Before the end of the first century (before the writing of John's Gospel—John 1 is probably a pre-Johannine hymn), the concept of the divine Logos stood ready and waiting as Christian thought turned to the question of the relationship of Jesus to the one he called "God" or "The Father."[89] From the time of John's Gospel up to the Council of Nicaea (325 A.D.) it is the ambiguous status of this Logos in respect to God or "the Father" which Christian thought tries to resolve. In terms of the requirements and possibilities of Greek thought of the fourth century, Nicaea gave the only answer reconcilable with the New Testament evidence. In a world where the requirements and possibilities are different, Nicaea's answer is largely unintelligi-

ble and the essential problem remains. Before turning to the
Nicene crisis and its resolution, it will be very useful to survey
the development of Christian reflection on the relationship of
God and the Logos from New Testament times to the eve of
Nicaea.

2.33 For the author of John 1, it is clear that the Logos is by no
means an intermediate being: not only is the Logos "in the
presence of God" (Jn 1:1) but "in the beginning . . . God was
the Logos" (*ibid.*) or, in the better translation of the New English
Bible: "What God was, the Logos was." Despite the evident
influence of Hellenism on Jewish thought in the centuries after
Alexander,[90] it is clear that the author of this hymn is not
thinking in the typically Greek (and essentially *non-dialectic* spatial) category of intermediate being, but rather in the Hebraic
category of *personal presence* (*pros ton theon*).[91] It was probably this
firm conviction of the presence of the Logos to or within God
(but a presence which falls short of absolute identification)[92]
which resulted in the first "stretching" of the concept of "God"
and made it possible for Ignatius of Antioch (died ca 107 A.D. as
a martyr in Rome) to use the word "God" as a predicate in
speaking of Jesus Christ.[93] The exact relationship of Ignatius to
the Johannine "school" or tradition and to the author of the
Fourth Gospel is not entirely clear but his dependence on both
is beyond doubt. What is striking about Ignatius is how modern
(in Nicene terms!) some of his formulations seem.[94] When we
read some of these statements about Jesus Christ, it is almost as
though Nicaea and the battles of the fourth century are long
past: the tone is calm and assured and it is clear to one and all
that to be a Christian is to acknowledge that no other than God
himself became manifest in Jesus Christ. The whole frame of
reference is, of course, different. Despite the evident influence
of Hellenism on his thought and expression, his view of God
and Christ is dynamic and historical and he is the last voice

during the whole patristic period of a Jewish-Christian orthodoxy whose full development might have prevented the raising
of unfortunate questions and the formulating of dangerous answers in the centuries that followed.[95] But, for the moment at
least, the future of Christian thought lay with Hellenism, and it
was forced to face the problem of the relation of the Logos to
God in typically Greek terms.

2.34   About the middle of the second century, a group of writers known as the Apologists (Justin the Martyr is the best
known) suggested that the Logos is in some way *in* Jesus. This
Logos was the *thought* of God, and as such it was the instrument
which he used in creation. The Apologists never really speak of
the Logos as a person—the Logos is rather the thought in which
God shows who he is—but even here the Logos is not precisely
God's thought of himself but rather his thought about what he
would create. As a result, for the Apologists, the procession or
"coming forth" of the Logos from God depends on creation.[96]
Toward the end of the same century, Irenaeus of Lyons returned consciously to the position of the prologue of John's
Gospel. For him, the Logos pre-exists creation and is not simply
in Jesus but is in some way *identified* with him. The Logos, which
had always existed, had manifested itself in a great variety of
ways since the beginning of the world. The incarnation is the
last of these manifestations, the most perfect and the definitive
one.

    This firm assertion that the Logos had always existed (and
therefore was "with God" since before the beginning) did succeed in breaking up the absolute and static unity of the Greek
concept of God, and it did this in the name of Scripture itself,
which knew only of a God who, while remaining the *wholly other,*
ineffable one, nevertheless chose not to remain alone but *engaged* himself and his power on behalf of that which was not.

2.35 But such a God is a paradox and such a statement is dialectical in the extreme—it contains elements which, in terms of human thought and discourse, are contradictory and which call for a resolution which is nothing less than a wholly new view of reality. However, the Greek mind was comfortable neither with the paradox nor with the dialectical methods of thought necessary to resolve it. Typically, instead of transcending paradox in a new unity, it sought to eliminate the paradox in a process of simplification and reduction. This simplification (pursued in the name of compromise or the "golden mean") could move in either of two directions: one of these emphasized the *unity* of God and the Logos (and practically eliminated distinction within God) and the other emphasized the *diversity* of God and Logos (and effectively made the Logos into a creature).

Those who emphasized the unity of God were called in the later tradition "monarchians"—a word which has little to do with "monarchy"in the modern sense, but refers to their insistence on the absolute oneness of the divine being which was the *principle* of all that existed (from *monē*, one and only, and *archē*, principle or beginning). One group of monarchians emphasized that the Logos and the Spirit were in God and existed in strict unity with him. For this group the Logos served to make creation a conceptual possibility, but could be of little help in understanding the relationship of Jesus with God. For them, Jesus was one who was *adopted* by the God who is the unique principle of all that is. In this act of adoption and in all that Jesus subsequently does, God *acts,* but only in and through this one who is distinct from him and in all essential respects *other.* *Adoptionism* has appeared in one form or another in most periods of Church history. It is a common form of reducing or eliminating the paradox of Jesus by raising the question of whether he is God *or* man and then deciding in favor of the second option. The first famous name associated with this type of Christology was that of Paul of Samosata, who was active about the year 250 A.D. For him there is one God who is the unique beginning, the absolute origin of all things, and this God acts by adopting Jesus as his Son and giving him the Spirit as a gift. Because of this emphasis on the *action* of God in adopting Jesus, Paul and his followers were called *dynamic monarchians.*

There was a second group of monarchians. Like the first they emphasized the absolute uniqueness of God, but they *identified* Christ with this unique principle. For them Christ was simply one of the ways or *modes* in which the absolutely one God appeared, and for this reason they are sometimes called *modalistic monarchians.* An alternate name and one which became common in the East was *Sabellians* (and their doctrine *Sabellianism*), after an individual named Sabellius who defended the teaching in Rome in the early 200's.

Two things should be noted about these early monarchians. First, they have taken the Greek notion of the God who is absolute unity, to whom all change and diversity is repugnant, and they have welded this to the New Testament concept of God as *Father,* interpreting this term not as referring to one who is in *dialogue* with another (the Son), but rather in terms of being the *source* or *origin* of all that is.[97] The second notable feature of this early monarchianism is that in typically Greek fashion, speculation centers on the divinity, on the uniqueness of the divine origin or first principle, and there is very little interest in the man, Jesus of Nazareth. Both forms of monarchianism tried to resolve the problem of the absolutely *one* God who intervened in the world of diversity and change by emphasizing the *oneness* of God and *limiting* the reality of his participation in the world. God and the Logos were rigorously one, and this absolute *One* was protected from all real involvement in the world.

However, there was a second way of grappling with the same problem: this was to emphasize the *distinction* between God and the Logos. According to this solution, God expresses or manifests himself, and this expression, idea, thought or word *shares his own being.* In the eastern provinces of the empire, where Greek patterns of thought were dominant, this approach was quite congenial. Philosophers had been accustomed for at least three centuries before Plotinus to approach the problem of relating the one God to the multiplicity of creation by means of a series of emanations, intermediate beings which proceeded from the divinity without lessening it but communicated a share in its reality to the material world. For Origen, the greatest theologian of the third century, the Logos exists because God begets or generates a "second God" (*deuteros theos*), who is the Word and who is in Christ. It would be difficult to imagine a clearer statement of the distinction between God and Logos, or one more threatening to the monotheism of both the Old Testament and the New.

Origen was active as a theologian from about 200 to 250 A.D., but before turning to the consequences of his thought and the influence he had on later generations, we have to cast a side glance at another very serious problem—a perennial one for Christology and one which has not really been solved up to the present day. The problem of unity and multiplicity in God immediately raises the same question in regard to Jesus Christ. More to the point: *the more firmly Jesus is located in the divine sphere, the less important his humanity becomes.* The more effective the "divinization" of Jesus (in the *Greek* sense of "divine"), the more irrevocable the split induced within the one Jesus Christ.

2.36 This process of de-emphasizing the role of the humanity of Jesus began in the eastern provinces, where Greek thought held sway, and proceeded with alarming rapidity. Already by the end of the second century, Clement of Alexandria (who was Origen's teacher) spoke of Jesus in a way which brings him close to docetism (from the Greek *dokein*, "seem"—the doctrine which asserted that Jesus Christ merely appeared or seemed to be human or that the Word did not really become man but merely took over a human nature as a kind of garb or vestment). Clement stated that Christ's *apatheia*—his essential immunity to all of the troubles and pains of limited human existence—was complete. Whether Clement believed that Jesus had a human soul is uncertain, but within the framework of his thought it would be almost impossible to find a role for such a human soul to play.[98] Origen would later argue that Christ's human soul had pre-existed its entry into the body, but the only function of such a soul was to unite the Logos with the flesh, the body of Jesus. Once this union had been effected, there remained no further role for it to play. In fact, for over a century after Origen's death, there was great hesitation throughout the East in regard to the human soul of Jesus. Since for Greek thought the soul is the formal and determining principle of a human being, there is no clearer indication of the difficulty that the Greek East experienced in affirming the real humanity, the true human-ness of Jesus. After Origen and well into the fourth century the problem with which theology struggled was again that of the relation of God to the Logos. Origen and his successors are agreed that Jesus Christ in some sense *is* the Logos, but this assertion which, abstractly considered, might be seen as a real advance in christological thought served, in the concrete, as a means of dehumanizing Jesus of Nazareth.[99]

2.37 As the fourth century began, theology in the eastern part of the empire attempted to solve the problem of the relation of God to the Logos by emphasizing one or the other side of Origen's legacy. If for Origen the Logos was *deuteros theos*—a second(ary) God—then two possibilities exist. Either the emphasis can be put on *theos*, and the Logos, although generated, is *eternally God* and has the existence which is proper to God, or the emphasis can be put on *deuteros* (which then comes to mean something more like "secondary") and the Logos is not God himself, but rather a secondary divine being. Origen's legacy was inherently unstable and the whole fourth century was to indicate how dangerous the situation was for the Church.

At this precise moment—in the year 318 A.D.—a priest of the diocese of Alexandria began to teach an especially radical form of the "secondary God" approach to the Logos. Arius was a logician and a rationalist, and his teaching had that simplicity about it which appeals to those who enjoy religious controversy and who especially enjoy scoring points in such confrontations. His teaching can be summarized quite adequately in three sentences (in itself not a very good sign): *God has no origin. The Word is generated—that is, the Word has an origin. Therefore, the Word is not God.* Arius' motto, and one which he never grew tired of reciting, was: "ēn pote hote ouk ēn," that is, "there was a time when he was not." Since he was something of a fundamentalist, Arius pounced gleefully on the not inconsiderable number of New Testament texts which emphasize the real humanity of Jesus— for example, Jn 17:3: ". . . you the one true God and Jesus Christ whom you have sent."

The threat posed by Arius was serious and the struggle which followed was a matter of life or death for the Church. The tragedy was not that orthodoxy lost the battle with Arianism but rather that orthodoxy won its victory on a terrain which had been staked out in the very terms which made the Arian heresy inevitable. Arius had brought into the open a problem which was latent in the Origenism of the East[100] and ultimately in the Greek idea of God—an idea which had never been adequately criticized in the name of the revelation of both the Old Testament and the New. As a result of this victory achieved on essentially alien terrain at Nicaea, the Church will approach with noticeable embarrassment or reserve all of those New Testament texts which indicate the dependence of Jesus on God or speak of his subordination to God. In time, apparently in the spirit of "building a fence around the law," this reserve will extend to all those texts which affirm the real humanity of Jesus and which accept without embarrassment his real subjection to all of the limitations of the human condition. As so often in the history of dogma, the victory of the Church over one heresy made the Church vulnerable to the opposite heresy—less, perhaps, on the theoretical level than on that of liturgy and popular piety, but no less damaging. When distortions of faith are clearly articulated, they can be criticized from the standpoint of the scriptural norm. When they lurk beneath the surface in popular catechetics and piety, they cannot be judged by the norm of Scripture but tend to create their own false context for the interpretation of Scripture. But this point will occupy our attention in a later chapter. At the moment we have to turn to that council which resolved the Arian problem in principle and to the stranger story of the fifty years of theological in-fighting which were needed before the council's victory was accepted throughout the Church.

2.4   The Council of Nicaea and Its Aftermath

In the years 312 and 313 A.D. Constantine had assumed control of the empire. Whatever else he may have thought of the God of the Christians and of Jesus Christ (under the standard of whose cross Rome's pagan armies now marched)[101] he saw one thing clearly: in an age in which separation of Church and state was inconceivable, he needed a faith to unite the empire. The strife caused by Arius' teaching, and by the vigorous opposition it called forth, had to be stopped. And to this end, Constantine summoned the bishops of the Church to assemble in a small town near his new imperial capitol in the spring of the year 325 A.D. There, prodded by the emperor (who had probably been convinced of the need to condemn Arius by his theological advisor, Hosius, bishop of Cordoba), the bishops adopted a strong anti-Arian formula which declares (*in the English translation*)[102] that Jesus Christ is "true God from true God, begotten not made." Here the terminology is still that of the New Testament, although the teaching evidently goes beyond explicit New Testament doctrine (precisely, as we will see, in extending or broadening the word "God" so that it not only included the one to whom Jesus speaks and whom he calls "Father," but also included *Jesus himself*, at least on one level or dimension of his being). But then the bishops at Nicaea, in order to clarify their view and to accede to Constantine's wish to condemn Arius unequivocally, further assert that Jesus Christ is (*English translation*) "consubstantial (or: *of one substance*) with the Father." The Greek term is worth knowing here: *homoousion tō patri*.

This is a fateful moment in the history of the Church. For the first time, a solemn assembly of the teaching Church adopts a non-scriptural term in order to safeguard and protect the teaching of Scripture itself. Beyond any doubt, the bishops succeeded in condemning Arius and his teaching, although subsequent events would suggest that their hearts may not have been in it and that they voted as they did out of either respect for or fear of the emperor. When allowance is made for this fact, what was their positive teaching?

2.41   First, except for Hosius and a few others, the bishops who met at Nicaea were all from the Greek-speaking East. Although the creed, the statement of faith which was issued at the end of their meetings, speaks of Jesus Christ, their real concern is with the *Logos* or *Word* of God. They are quite clear that the Logos became man, but it is the relation of this Logos to the Father which demands their attention.

Second, they used the word "God" in a way which is nothing less than a fateful departure from New Testament terminology, although it can be easily missed. "God" in the Nicene creed is no longer solely the Father of Jesus Christ (this is the New Testament usage),[103] but has become a name or designation which applies *both* to the Father *and* to the Logos or Son. The word has been expanded or stretched and is well on the way to a new meaning—it will refer not to what is *personal* in God but rather to the *qualities* or *attributes* of divine being.

Third, the bishops at Nicaea were probably convinced that redemption was essentially a raising of man to a share in the divine life and that Jesus had to have this life as his own if he were to be Redeemer in the true and proper sense. (There was a strong Platonic flavor to this view. Human nature is thought of as being *one,* almost like a Platonic form. In Jesus, one human nature is brought into contact with divinity, and therefore the divine power suffuses all who share in this nature. For such a theology the incarnation is the essential redemptive event, not the cross.)[104]

Finally, the bishops almost certainly meant by their *homoousion* formula to assert that the Logos or Son was fully divine (which for them meant, above all, *immutable* and *eternal*). However, it is unlikely that many of them understood by this that the Logos was *identical* in substance with the Father. Terminology was not yet sufficiently refined for them to make this distinction. There were clearly certain implications in what the Council of Nicaea decreed, which many or most of those present did not see. Those who did see them with some clarity were the very ones who opposed the Nicene teaching and who fought more or less openly during the next fifty years for the Arian doctrine. More than once during this half century it looked as though they might win. Since the struggle then and for the next three centuries was really about the terminology used to speak of God, the Logos and Jesus, it will be useful to pause briefly here and define the principal terms used.[105]

2.42   Excursus: The Problem of Terminology

There is a general problem of terminology which is encountered everywhere in philosophy and theology and in the natural and human sciences as well: human language evolved in order to permit primitive people to deal with the practical tasks of life—cooperation in hunting and foraging probably played a major role here. In virtue of this origin, language is suitable for dealing with things which can be seen, heard, felt, handled and eaten—that is, with reality as tangible and apparent. In itself it is not very suited for dealing with the intangible and with reality which underlies the apparent. In attempting to speak of the deeply real and of that which *is* and does not merely seem to be, language will always use words which are designed to speak of space and time and of the events which take place there. Language can only speak of the invisible and intangible in terms of the visible and tangible. Language is *essentially metaphorical.*

Since the seventh century B.C., the Greeks had been engaged in pushing forward the frontiers of thought and therefore of language. They asked probing questions about their world and its origins. They thought deeply about the fact that things often were not really what they seemed to be and they asked what the *really real* was. From the Greek verb *to be* (*einai*) they created an abstract noun (*ousia*) which meant the reality of a thing (or person)—that which something really is, as distinct from what it seems or appears to be. A good paraphrase in English would be: *what someone or something really is.* Another word with similar meaning was derived from the verb which meant *to grow* (*phyein*); it was the nominal form (*physis*) which played an important role in the christological struggles of the fifth century. Like *ousia* it means the *reality of a thing,* particularly *that underlying reality which is the source of growth and activity.*

A third word was used which had, at least when it first appeared, a very similar meaning. This was the word *hypostasis*—

literally, *a standing under.* This, too, referred to the *deep reality* of a thing or person. It was for all practical purposes a synonym of both *ousia* and *physis.* This usage, which did not distinguish these three words, continued throughout the fourth century and well into the fifth. When the Romans became interested in philosophy in the first century B.C. they translated the Greek word *hypostasis* element by element into Latin and got *substantia.* Although in time the meaning of *hypostasis* changed, *substantia* kept its original meaning as long as Latin continued to be used in philosophy and theology—that is, the deep, underlying reality of a thing or person. Latin also had a word which had almost the exact shading of the Greek *physis*—that is, *natura,* the reality of a thing precisely insofar as it is viewed as the *principle of activity.*

The three Greek terms mentioned so far: *ousia, hypostasis,* and *physis*—all meant the *reality* of a thing or person. But at least in pre-Christian Greek thought, this "reality" was understood in a characteristically Platonic fashion—it was the universally valid idea of a thing or person, that which was shared by all the individuals who participated in this universal idea or form. However, Christianity had brought a new sense of the uniqueness. the dignity and the value of the individual human being. For the New Testament, men are not replicas of a single divine idea, but individuals, addressed by God, for whom Christ died and who are called as individuals to accept the good news and to begin an eternal relationship with God who had from the beginning "loved them with an everlasting love."[106]

The individual person, although something of a stepchild in Greek philosophy, was more acceptable in popular thought, and both the Greek and Latin words for the individual human being have a distinctly unphilosophical ring. The Greek *prosōpon* (it originally meant *face*) and the Latin *persona* (originally the *mask* which distinguished one actor from another in the drama) came to mean the *concrete, individual reality of the human being.* As such, these words refer not to *what one is* (which one shares, of course, with all other members of the human race), but rather to *who* one is. The Greek and Latin words are not too far in meaning from the English word *person* as we will later define it, and the hesitation in the use of these words to speak of Father, Son, and Spirit which we find in the work of the best theologians of the East and the West, is a fact of which too little notice has been taken.

In the years around and after 300 A.D., theologians who confronted the old task of speaking of a God who was at once transcendent to the world and immanent within it began to develop a new terminology—one which allowed them to speak of distinctions within the divine life or divine nature. Instead of coining a new word, they took the old word *hypostasis* which had been a synonym of *ousia* and referred to the underlying reality of a thing and they gave it a new meaning. Instead of referring to the underlying reality of a thing or person, that which a thing or person is, it came to mean *the way in which this underlying reality is possessed.*[107] In itself, *hypostasis* simply means this—*a principle of distinction within the deep, underlying reality of a thing.* Such a concept is, of course, highly formal—it says nothing about the type or character of the distinction but merely asserts that there is a distinction. It was nevertheless a useful concept because it gave the Greek mind which was unsympathetic to dialectical thought a way of dealing with the apparent contradictions in the divine essence. But it was a concept which would in time cause a great deal of trouble, particularly when translated into Latin and into the modern languages. Although we will discuss the matter more thoroughly in a later chapter, the problem must at least be mentioned here in this initial survey of terminology.

When *hypostasis* came to be differentiated from *ousia* and to have a new meaning—the way in which the underlying reality of a thing is possessed—this came about because of the need to find a distinction within the life of God, for reasons we have already seen. Now although pre-Christian Greek thought seemed comfortable with a "god" who is something other than personal, Christian thought, even when much influenced by the philosophical tradition, could not be satisfied with an impersonal "god." The God of both the Old Testament and the New is evidently a God who knows and loves, who is free in choice and action, and it is impossible to think of the knowledge, love and freedom of such a God without using human knowledge, love and freedom as *models*. This is not only inevitable; it is a good way to talk about God. In fact, I would argue that to take the mystery of human intelligence and love and freedom seriously is already to have encountered God. However, precisely at this juncture, Greek patterns of thought were problematic. The *ousia*, the deep underlying reality which was the *model* for man's understanding of the *ousia*, the deep, underlying reality of God, was precisely the human *ousia*—that universal intelligibility which all human beings possess. Now what distinguishes and differentiates this universal humanity in each individual is that each of us is a *distinct subject*, a different "one who" knows and loves, a distinct and conscious possessor of the common nature. For *us*, distinction within the common nature (as the Greek mind saw it) is effected by the fact that each of us is a distinct "*someone*" who knows and loves. Therefore, it was easy for the word which, in itself, meant only a *way of possessing underlying reality* to acquire a new meaning: *a distinct conscious subject of knowing and willing*. When this change of meaning takes place, the assertion that there is more than one *hypostasis* in God is equivalent to the assertion that there is more than one *personal subject* (that is, *person* in the *modern* sense) in God.

At least on the level of terminology, Greek thought did not take this step. *Hypostasis* continued to be used to speak of that which is distinct in God, and the other word *prosōpon* (which corresponds rather closely to the modern word *person*) was, in general (outside Nestorianism), not used to speak of this distinction. Of course, for the reasons outlined in the last paragraph, people came to think of the three *hypostaseis* in God as *three distinct conscious subjects,* but as long as the highly technical word *hypostasis* was used, such ways of thinking could always be criticized from the vantage point of Scripture.

However, Latin theology did not enjoy this advantage, because the Latin language of the time used the one word *persona* to translate both *prosōpon* and *hypostasis.* Augustine saw the danger this entailed and had grave doubts about the propriety of using *persona* to designate the distinctions in God—that is, whatever there are three of in God,[108] but by his time the term *persona* was already accepted and there was little he could do. It was at a much later point in the history of Western theology that a new term was developed to translate the Greek *hypostasis* in the latter's sense of *way of possessing underlying reality* or *principle of distinction.* Unfortunately this new word—*subsistentia*—was not available in Augustine's day or before. The consequences of using the modern derivatives of Latin *persona* (English: person; German: Person; French: personne; Spanish and Italian: persona) to translate the Latin word in theological writing and in professions of faith will be treated at some length in a later chapter. For the moment we will return to the period immediately after the Council of Nicaea and then comment briefly on the events of the next fifty-six years.

2.43 It was probably evident to many of the bishops when they arrived in their home dioceses after leaving Nicaea that the council had gone much farther than many of them or their clergy wished to go. Not that it had gone too far in affirming what we would call today the divinity of the Logos or Son; most of them were convinced of this before they arrived at Nicaea. The problem was that the council had gone much farther in the direction of affirming the *unity* of God than the Greek East was prepared to go. Naturally, it was the word *homoousion* (which affirmed identity of substance, underlying reality, in the Father and the Logos or Son) which would come under attack, and this word played the major role in the theological debates of the next half century.

As long as Constantine was alive no one dared question the *homoousion* formula, and so for twelve years the opponents of Nicaea tried to undermine the council indirectly by attacking those bishops who were known to be supporters of the consubstantiality of Father and Son (or Word). Two bishops, both named Eusebius, were particularly effective here: Eusebius of Nicomedia in the political arena, and Eusebius of Caesarea, whose work as the first Church historian gave his theological opinions a prestige which they did not merit on strictly theological grounds. The views of the bishop of Caesarea are worth a brief note here because they can give us some insight into why opposition to Nicaea was so impassioned on the part of many sincere Christians. His position can be summarized in four points. First, Eusebius felt, along with many other Church Fathers who were influenced by middle Platonism, that distinctions within God were absolutely necessary in order to safeguard the divine transcendence. Accordingly, he insisted on the fact that the Logos or Son has his own *hypostasis,* which *at the time* meant his own *distinct existence.*[109] Second, although the Word or Son was not created, he was begotten and was therefore *not eternal* in the same sense as the Father. (Note here again that any form of *becoming* or *coming to be* has to be excluded from the life of the one who is God in the most strict and absolute sense of the word—that is, the Father.) Third, Eusebius saw in the term *homoousios* a direct assault on the real distinction of Father and Son which alone could preserve the divinity from contamination by the world of changing things. Fourth and last, in Eusebius' view, Christ stands over against the Father precisely as Logos or Word and *not as man.* Like so many others of his day for a century before and after his time, Eusebius had no place for a human soul in Christ, no room for an essentially human spontaneity. We will return now to the years which followed the council of Nicaea.

Constantine died in 337, and on his death the empire was divided among three of his sons, with Constantius exercising power throughout the East. Constantius' sympathies were Arian, and he did what he could to encourage opposition to Nicaea, but he did so cautiously, because he was not sole ruler. By the year 351 his other brothers had been killed and Constantius ruled alone. The mask was cast aside and the opposition to Nicaea which had been fermenting since 325 emerged into the open. In one synod (local council) after another, the *homoousion* formula was rejected and it seemed that throughout the empire Arianism was supreme.

However, it was precisely the apparent victory of this rather crude Arianism which led the more moderate opponents of Nicaea to re-examine their positions. Athanasius of Alexandria (who spent a considerable portion of his life in exile because of his forceful defense of Nicaea) was tireless in attempting to win the moderate anti-Nicene party over to the doctrine of the council. Because he was not only tireless but patient and understanding, he succeeded in convincing the moderates of the opposing party of the danger of saying that the Son was not identical in substance with the Father, but only of *like* or *similar substance.* (From the Greek word for similar—*homoios*—came the name of this moderate anti-Nicene group: they were called *homoeoousians.*) This gradual victory of Nicaea, at precisely the moment when all seemed lost, took place between the years 361 (the death of Constantius) and 381. The victory was sealed at the First Council of Constantinople in the year 381: Nicaea was affirmed and the *homoousion* was extended to a third hypostasis in God—the Spirit. Arianism as such posed no further threat after the First Council of Constantinople, but, as noted above, the triumph of the Nicene orthodoxy had been won on a terrain marked by typically Greek questions and problems. In the strug-

gle with Arianism the Church had played down to some degree
the humanity of Jesus Christ, and on the level of popular piety
the Church forever after was to exhibit a certain embarrassment
at the fact that God chose to turn a truly human face to the
world in Jesus.[110]

2.5   Christology after Nicaea

Nicaea had affirmed that Christ was *homoousion,* of one
substance, with the Father. From the New Testament tradition it
was clear (at least formally, in theory) that Jesus was *homoousion*
with us (that is, that he possessed the same nature or substance
as we do). He is therefore in some sense both God and man.
The attempt to grasp both the possibility and the fact of Jesus'
being God and man occupied theology in the eastern part of the
empire for the next one hundred and twenty-five years. Toward
the end of this period, the West became involved in the dispute,
and Rome intervened decisively.

2.51   The first attempt to deal with the paradox of the man who
is God is associated with the city of Alexandria and is called the
Logos-Sarx or *Word-Flesh* Christology. According to this approach, in Jesus the Logos was united not really with a *man,* in
the sense of a *complete and integral human nature,* but rather simply
with *flesh,* that is, with a *human body.* In terms of the philosophy
of the time, since a complete human nature included both body
and soul, the proponents of Logos-Sarx argued that Jesus must
not have had a human soul and that for him the Logos played
the role which the human soul does in other members of our
race.

At this period, the Logos-Sarx christology is found explicitly only in the work of Apollinaris, bishop of Laodicea (his dates:
ca. 310 to 390). Apollinaris asserted that the Word takes the
place of a human soul in Christ and that the result of this event

is *the one incarnate nature of the divine Word.* (Remember this phrase: it will be attributed to Athanasius and it will cause difficulties which the Eastern Church never successfully resolved.)

It was typical of the Church in the patristic period that its critique of Apollinaris was more Platonic than scriptural in its inspiration. No one seemed to object to the fact that a man without a soul was, in terms of the philosophy of the time, something less than a man.[111] What did make Apollinaris' teaching suspect to many of his contemporaries was the fact that it called into question the *divinization* of man which had been effected by the union of the Logos with *human nature* in Jesus Christ. Gregory of Nazianzus pointed this out about the year 370 and coined a famous phrase: "What has not been assumed has not been restored; it is what is united with God which is saved."[112] At least from the Greek point of view, Gregory had isolated the weakness of Apollinaris' position, and his teaching was condemned at a series of synods in the East in the late fourth century.

Although Apollinaris was the only one to teach the Logos-Sarx Christology in this extreme form, the theologians of the city of Alexandria, while usually not denying that there was a human soul in Christ, never seemed capable of taking that soul seriously or of finding a role for the human soul of Jesus to play. Already in 180 A.D. Clement, Origen's teacher, spoke of the *apatheia* of Jesus, his immunity to the limitations of human existence, in a way which sounds docetic and seems to make of the humanity of Jesus little more than the garb worn by a divine being who appears in the world. Athanasius spoke of Jesus "pretending"[113] weakness and ignorance in a way which clearly prefigured the threat posed to the humanity of Jesus by the Nicene victory—a threat which is as real today as it was sixteen hundred years ago. Alexandria always emphasized the *unity* of Jesus Christ, and this was the source of its theological strength;

but this emphasis on unity, when joined with the typically Greek inability to take the man Jesus very seriously, led to a unity which was due entirely to the informing, directing and controlling power of the Logos. Developments at Chalcedon and after simply transferred this Alexandrine emphasis on the dominant role of the Logos in Jesus to another level and expressed it in different terms. In this latter form, the triumph of Alexandria has led to a dehumanizing of Jesus which has been able to coexist quite well with verbal orthodoxy up to the present day.

2.52 The second attempt to link God and man in Jesus is associated with the city of Antioch in Syria and is usually called a *Logos-Anthropos* or *Word-Man* Christology. According to this view, the Logos or Word was not united with a mere body or with flesh alone but with a *full and complete man*. The theologians of Antioch attempted in at least one respect to take the evidence of the Gospels seriously. They saw that the subjection of Jesus to the limitations and the brokenness of human existence was real, and not a matter of pretense or gifted acting.

Theodore of Mopsuestia (ca. 350 to 428) gives us a good example of this Christology. According to him, the word assumed a *man* with body and soul, because this is the only way in which Jesus could be said to possess full human reality. When the question of how the unity of Jesus could be maintained under such circumstances was raised, Theodore answered that a *single person*[114] *resulted from the coming together of the two natures.* Theodore was evidently not willing to say that the *Logos* was the person who was the acting subject in each of these two natures.

2.6 Ephesus and the Road to Chalcedon

Antioch and Alexandria were not only theological rivals but political rivals as well. Both rivalries led to an open break when Cyril became bishop of Alexandria and Nestorius, from the diocese of Antioch, became patriarch of the capital city of Constantinople—the latter on April 10 of the year 428. Nestorius was not much of a theologian, and in addition he had a gift for saying the wrong thing at the wrong time to the wrong audience. No sooner had he mounted the episcopal throne than he began using the prestige of his new office to press the Antiochene solution to the God-man dilemma. Nestorius seems to have developed the Logos-Anthropos Christology in somewhat radical form, although there is good evidence that he was far more orthodox than he was thought to be at the time and for centuries after his death.[115] His teaching can be summarized in these five points.

First (in a move calculated to infuriate the monastic communities of both Constantinople and Egypt—in both of these places Marian piety was strong) Nestorius taught that Mary was not *theotokos* (Mother of God) but *christotokos* (mother of Christ), and the latter title meant for Nestorius "mother of the *man* Jesus Christ." This led many of his contemporaries to think that he was asserting the existence of two persons, two subjects in Christ, although it seems clear that this was not the case. Second, the two natures of Christ remain unchanged and distinct, even when they come together in Jesus. The Word, of course, cannot change (Nestorius was just as "Greek" as his opponents in this respect), but on the other hand, Christ is genuinely human, and the only way to safeguard the truth of both of these statements is to assert the abiding distinction of the two natures. Third, each nature has its own *prosopon* or *hypostasis*. In saying this, Nestorius seems to mean simply that each nature has its own *objective reality,* and he seems to use *hypostasis* as a synonym of *prosopon*—that is, the objective reality of a thing precisely as *evident,* as *manifest.*[116] Fourth, the natures are not really united but merely *joined together* in what Nestorius called a *prosopon of union,* by which he apparently meant simply the *de facto union* of God and man in Christ, or the *objective reality of Christ.* Fifth,

Nestorius did not say anything about the *person* of Jesus and about what constituted that personhood.

As patriarch of Alexandria, Cyril defended an orthodox form of the Logos-Sarx Christology of his native city. He did not deny the existence of a human soul in Jesus Christ, but he strongly emphasized the unity of the God-man and he understood this unity as something effected by the Logos or Word. For Cyril, Nestorius' view that the two natures in Christ were simply *joined together* was blatant heresy for two reasons: first, it divided the one Jesus Christ, and, second, it allowed some of Jesus' actions (specifically his death on the cross) to be the actions of man and not of God. In Cyril's view, unless the cross is the suffering of God, it is without power to save us.

The struggle between Cyril and Nestorius showed something important about the long dispute between Alexandria and Antioch: they differed not because they gave different answers to the same question; rather, they asked quite different questions because they framed the problem of the God-man in different terms. For the Antiochenes, the problem of speculative Christology was that of explaining how two real and distinct natures came together and were united in the one concrete being, Jesus Christ. For the Alexandrines the problem was that of explaining how the Logos, who had existed from all eternity within the divine life, could in time take upon himself a human way of acting. Antioch started with the duality of the natures of Christ, Alexandria with the unity of subject.

2.61 In the year 430 Cyril wrote to the Pope (Celestine) to inform him that Nestorius was teaching that the Virgin was not properly speaking the Mother of God and to ask that he be condemned for teachings contrary to the traditional faith. Celestine agreed with Cyril and defended the title *theotokos.* He gave Nestorius ten days to recant and commissioned Cyril as executor of the papal decree. Cyril was delighted and took his appointment very seriously. He composed a list of ten anathemas (condemned propositions) and submitted them to Nestorius with orders to sign them (that is, to join Cyril in condemning them). These anathemas were so typically Alexandrine in phraseology that they shocked the *moderate* members of the Antiochene party (of which Nestorius was, verbally at least, a radical member). What the moderates found particularly repugnant was Cyril's speaking of the "one nature of the Incarnate Word"—a formula which he and the other Alexandrines erroneously attributed to Athanasius, but which actually went back to Apollinaris.

In order to settle the dispute, a council was called to the city of Ephesus in the summer of 431. There, on June 22 (before the bishops from Antioch and the other dioceses which depended on that city had arrived), Cyril met with other bishops of his own party and excommunicated Nestorius. The commissioners of the emperor objected to this high-handed move, but this was the "council" which was approved by the legates of the Pope on July 10 of the same year, and it is the one which has gone down in history as the third ecumenical council. (By this time, Nestorius had also met with his supporters—on June 26—and excommunicated Cyril, but this meeting was not recognized by the papal legates.)

Two of the major sees of Christendom had now excommunicated each other, and the task of restoring union was a pressing one for both the Church and the empire. There were two major obstacles: Cyril's list of anathemas (which went much farther in the direction of affirming the unity of the God-man than the moderate bishops of Antiochene persuasion were willing to go), and the excommunication of Nestorius, which the Antiochenes regarded as a personal insult.

Surprisingly, in the year 433 a compromise was achieved through the work of Bishop John of Antioch and Cyril of Alexandria. Cyril "explained" his anathemas to the Antiochene party—after that time he seems to have made no use of them—and, on the other side, the Antiochenes dropped Nestorius and agreed to his excommunication. This important agreement was sealed in a document which is called the *Symbol of Union*, which took the form of a letter of John of Antioch to Cyril.

2.7   En Route Toward Chalcedon

The Symbol of Union really interpreted Ephesus in a way which the Antiochene party could accept, and if Cyril had lived longer the theology of the East might have been able to work toward a new christological synthesis without the pressures created by imperial and ecclesiastical politics. But Cyril died in 444 and his more radical followers, who saw in the Symbol of Union nothing less than a betrayal of Alexandrine theology and therefore of the faith itself, gathered around Dioscuros, the new bishop. This group was looking for an opportunity to reverse the compromise effected by the Symbol of Union and to reaffirm the anathemas (which Cyril had withdrawn in his agreement with John of Antioch). This opportunity was offered to them in 448 when open opposition to the Symbol of Union flared in some of the monastic communities of Constantinople.[117] The dissidents gathered around an elderly monk by the name of Eutyches—a man whose apparent piety had given him considerable influence with the emperor's family, but whose theological views could at best be called confused. What Eutyches held was an exaggerated version of the old Alexandrine Logos-Sarx theology—he was convinced that Jesus' humanity had been *absorbed* into his divinity. Reports were sent to Rome concerning Eutyches' teaching, and on June 13, 449 Leo, the Pope at the time, wrote a letter to Flavian, bishop of Constantinople, in which he condemned Eutyches and explained the doctrine of the two natures, as this had been elaborated in the Western Church (and was widely accepted for more than a century before the dispute in question). In the same year, in order to re-establish union in the empire, the emperor Theodosius II directed the bishops to assemble again for a council in the city of Ephesus. In August 449, a group of bishops under the leadership of Dioscuros, Cyril's successor, met in Ephesus. At this meeting (the results of which were accepted by the imperial commissioners) Dioscuros took complete control, refused to allow the reading of Leo's letter to Flavian, and rehabilitated Eutyches. The Pope and the emperor were now on different sides.

The impasse was broken several months later when, on July 28, 450, Theodosius fell off his horse and died of a broken back. The new emperor, Marcian, quickly called for a council to meet the following year in Chalcedon.

2.8 The Council of Chalcedon

On October 8, 451 about five hundred bishops met in Chalcedon. From the very beginning of the council, the imperial commissioners insisted that the assembled bishops agree on a formula which all participants could sign, thus restoring religious unity to the empire. As it turned out, the essential elements of this formula came from Leo's letter to Flavian of June 13, 449. In addition to reaffirming Nicaea, there are two central points in Leo's teaching: first, in Jesus Christ there are two distinct *principles of operation,* which coexist without mixture (that is, which remain distinct). In Latin, the word for these principles of operation was *naturae,* translated into Greek as *physeis* (and transliterated into English as *nature,* although it has little to do with the use of this term in contemporary language). Second, Leo insisted that there is only one acting *subject* in Jesus Christ and that this subject is the Logos or Word. Since the Word is the ultimate subject in Jesus, it is correct to say such things as "the Word suffered" and "Mary is the Mother of God." For the acting subject in Jesus Christ, Leo used the Latin term which had been used all along to translate the Greek "hypostasis"—that is, *persona*. This term has been transliterated into English as *person*—perhaps the most questionable translation ever made of a dogmatic formula.

The Council of Chalcedon was a strong and clear restatement of the same theology which Cyril and John of Antioch had agreed on in their Symbol of Union, but for precisely this reason it seemed to the radical Alexandrine group in 451 to be nothing short of a sell-out to Antiochene heresy. For purely political reasons (to secure the loyalty of Alexandria and of those dioceses of the East which depended on it), the Church of Constantinople, always vulnerable to direct meddling on the part of the emperor, spent the next one hundred and fifty years trying to water down the dogmatic statements of Chalcedon where these touched on the abiding distinction of natures in Christ, or trying to make Chalcedon more palatable by condemning various theologians of the Antiochene school. Eventually the sorry spectacle terminated in failure, and Alexandria and several of the eastern provinces drifted off into the heresy of *monophysitism*—the belief that, at least after the incarnation, there is only one nature in Jesus Christ, that of the divine Word.

2.9   Chalcedon in Retrospect

Chalcedon was a compromise between two different schools of thought, which approached the problem of Jesus Christ in two entirely different ways. Alexandria saw the Logos as the principle of all the activity of Jesus Christ and tried to develop ways of speaking of how the pre-existent Logos became man, lived a truly human life, and then returned to the place from which he had come. Antioch was impressed by the obvious humanity of the Jesus of the Gospels while remaining convinced of his divinity and tried to develop ways of expressing the unity of Jesus Christ while holding firmly to the real distinction of being and powers in him.

If the two schools had simply used different terminology the problem would have been serious enough, but frequently they used the same terminology but meant different things—a fact which made misunderstanding inevitable. Most critical was the difference in meaning in respect to the words *prosopon* or *hypostasis*. For the Alexandrines these terms referred to the "who" of Jesus Christ, to the *ultimate acting subject*. For the Antiochenes they meant the *concrete, objective reality of each of the principles of activity* in Jesus Christ. Chalcedon owed its success not least to the fact that it regulated the way Christians were to *talk* about Jesus Christ—it imposed on Christians certain *linguistic conventions,* certain *norms of terminology.*[118]

By the year 451 there was nothing new in such a procedure—Nicaea, First Constantinople and Ephesus had all imposed such linguistic conventions on the Church—and this very fact suggests a way of assessing the role these councils should play in the faith of the Christian today and the way of achieving a freedom *from* them in one respect, which is a freedom *for* them in another. Linguistic conventions and terminological norms are not only valuable but probably necessary if the substance of Christian faith is to be affirmed without distortion or error *in a given language or linguistic context.* (The word "language" here is used in the same sense as in the first chapter: not simply the grammar and vocabulary of a foreign tongue, but the world-view and resources of thought and expression of a foreign place and time.) What Chalcedon and its predecessors assert is that when questions about Jesus Christ are raised in terms of *physis, ousia* and *hypostasis* (and the Latin equivalents *natura, substantia* and *persona*), then the answers contained in the dogmatic constitutions of those councils between the years 325 and 451 must be given. None of these councils affirmed that these ways of speaking were simply the best (or the only) ways of speaking; this was a possibility which they did not address because they could not envision it.

There is one more thing which the councils did not assert and which is of extreme importance: the councils did not really assert that Jesus Christ is "of one substance with the Father" or that in him there are "two natures and one person." These are English words, and the last of the councils in question was over for almost a thousand years before anything very similar to modern English was spoken on the earth. This is no trivial point: fifteen hundred and more years and several epoch-making shifts in man's view of himself and his world have endowed the modern words with meanings unsuspected by the bishops who assembled in the long-forgotten towns of the late ancient world. Statements *can* be intelligible and true only within the framework of a given language. For various reasons I believe that a cogent argument can be made in favor of both the intelligibility and the truth of the dogmas from Nicaea to Chalcedon[119] in terms of the language which was used then. If this is understood, these councils will be fruitful both for faith and for the understanding which proceeds from it. On the other hand, to demand that we accept the philosophical and anthropological suppositions of fifth century Greeks as a condition of possessing living faith today is worse than a mere anachronism, for it implicitly denies that Jesus and his word transcend the resources of all language and all time.

The Early Councils and the Problem of Christology Today

The task of speculative Christology today is not that of fashioning a conceptual apparatus and vocabulary of ever-increasing subtlety in order to cater to the tastes and needs of those for whom "simple faith" is not enough. Unless the faith in question is an act of understanding it does not merit the name "faith" and it should be unmasked as the destructive parody which it is. And unless theology (and therefore Christology) is an extension and prolongation of faith, then it should not be called theology but intellectual game-playing—a sport which in its proper place can be great fun, but which has little or nothing to do with our situation before God.

Furthermore, it is at least not the primary task of speculative Christology to attempt to understand what was said about Jesus Christ, his humanity and his divinity, by the early councils from Nicaea to Chalcedon. To see this as the task of reflection about Jesus today is to misunderstand the role these councils should play in Christian faith. They are not sources and they should never be allowed to eclipse the absolute primacy of Scripture in this respect. If the role of the councils is seen to be that of establishing binding norms of expression, valid linguistic conventions for those who can or must use a certain language in talking about Jesus Christ, they have an important contribution to make to faith, not least in showing that the real Jesus always transcends the attempt of any age to grasp and hold him in its categories of thought and expression.

The task of speculative Christology is to aid faith by helping it to be an act of understanding which is deep and transforming, and it will succeed in this task to the degree to which it helps believers to see exactly what they are called upon to believe— that is, to the degree to which it indicates what the real paradox and scandal of Jesus Christ is and to the degree to which it frees faith from the false scandal of a Jesus who never existed. This book is being written out of the conviction that the faith of many intelligent and sincere Christians today is deprived of transforming power in their lives, not because they lack the brilliance or subtlety to penetrate to the heart of the mystery of Jesus but because they feel obliged to believe things about Jesus which run counter to their deepest instincts about the real meaning of Jesus Christ in their lives. The doubts that many people today feel in regard to the traditional "dogmatic Christ" do not spring from a lack of faith. They are rooted in the conviction that the traditional dogmas, while formally true, at least sometimes stand in the way of knowing and loving the real Jesus and that they therefore fail, *precisely as dogma*. It will be worth our while to pause here and describe this malaise.

3.1   The Crisis of Christology Today

Many people today, even outside the traditional Churches, have a sense of the challenge of Jesus. Even in the somewhat old-fashioned words of the Gospel translations we can sense his power. We are drawn by his mystery and his words have a strange capacity to touch us. This man was so vulnerable, and he was ultimately broken by his enemies and rejected by the world, and yet he "taught with authority" then, and today his words still have the power to bring us life and peace.

It is this *man* Jesus, in the concreteness of the Gospel picture, who draws us to himself. The evident attractiveness belongs to the man himself and has nothing to do with the fact that people tell us that "he is God." Quite the opposite is the case. The fact that he might be God creates problems as soon as we hear it, because it seems to call into question the genuinity of the man, his human authenticity. Is this human being only a mask or facade for God? Is he vulnerable only in appearance? Is his weakness only a pretense? When he finally dies, apparently as a broken man, what have we seen? Was it a skillful piece of acting? Such a thought is appalling.

The statement that "Jesus is God" is presented not just as the view of a sect or a theological school. Rather, together with a number of similar statements, it confronts us as *dogma*—the solemn and binding teaching of the Church which protects the scriptural message from distortion and misunderstanding. But in regard to Jesus, so many of these dogmas seem to blunt his challenge and to mute his call. As we read the pronouncements of the councils from Nicaea to Chalcedon, can we overlook the insinuation that this Jesus who appeared to be a weak and broken man who died a failure is really, "underneath," the all-powerful God? Don't these documents—particularly those of Chalcedon—suggest that *Jesus is not a human person* at all, but the eternal second person of the Trinity, who now exists in, works through, uses a human nature, while keeping his divine nature intact? Isn't it evident that this Jesus knows all that has ever happened and all that will ever happen, even though he may conscientiously distinguish what he knows as God from what he knows as man? Isn't it precisely these questions which the dogmas of Nicaea, Constantinople, Ephesus and Chalcedon force us to raise? Greek Christians were enthralled in those days by the thought that in the Christ the divine and the human had met and that in him the corruptibility of the flesh had been overcome. But we are different. We are disappointed at the thought that one who appeared to be a human person was not one in reality, the thought that the history of Jesus was really nothing but the manifestation of a changeless God, the acting out of a drama

whose script was written in eternity. Despite the apparent grandeur which is accorded him, such a divinity seems poor compensation for that man, that human person, who shares our
uncertainty, our ignorance, our fragility—who was touched by a
sense of meaninglessness and despair and who died broken and
a failure.

We feel this all the more poignantly today, because we live
at a time when better ways of reading and understanding the
Gospels are available. The critical and historical study of the
stories about him reveal more clearly than ever before the
paradox of strength in weakness which is the mystery of the man
from Nazareth. The real Jesus has emerged from behind the
pious painting and has proven to be infinitely more attractive.
That this broken man now lives forever, that the iron laws of
fate have been shattered—this is the incredible good news we
long to believe, and the power of his words and his person is a
strong motive for this belief today. But the doubts keep returning: Is there anything wonderful about a God who lives forever?
If I look for a human person here and find only the garb and
mask of divinity, can there be any greater disappointment?

3.2 The Conciliar Teaching

These are the problems which the dogmas *seem* to pose. At
least superficially we seem to face a choice between the Jesus of
the Gospels and the Christ of the dogmas, who is also the Christ
of the Church. My contention is that this choice is precisely
that—superficial—because the dogmas of the early Church have
been much oversimplified. They have been read with insuffi-
cient attention to their purpose and to the totally different
situation of the Church which they addressed.

The dogmas in question here all deal directly or indirectly
with the relationship of Jesus Christ to one whom they call
"God." The councils had to face this question because the Jesus

of the Gospels repeatedly asserted a unique closeness, a real oneness with one whom he called "God" or "Father." (Jesus' contemporaries also used the word "God" in their prayers and religious disputes, but there is much evidence in the Gospels that he had reservations about their use of the word and that he distanced himself from their understanding.)[120] The early councils of the Church recognized that the relationship of Jesus to the one he called "God" or "Father" was the key to his mystery and his identity and to the urgency of his call.[121]

3.21 The dogmas are an attempt to speak accurately about this relationship and they do it as follows. The first group of statements concerns God: God is one in essence or nature and threefold in person. All the persons are of one substance or nature. There are three persons in one God and they are the Father, the Son and the Spirit. The development of these dogmatic statements was the work of the fourth century—it began at Nicaea and was completed by the time of First Constantinople in the year 381.[122] The second group of statements concerns Jesus Christ: He is the Son of God, one person in two natures. In his divinity he is begotten of the Father before time. In his humanity he is begotten of the Virgin Mary, who is therefore the Mother of God. The selfsame Christ must be acknowledged in two natures, without commingling, change, division or separation. The distinction between the natures is in no way removed by their union, but the specific character of each nature is preserved, and they are united in one person and one hypostasis.[123] The Son of God, descending from his heavenly throne, yet not leaving the glory of the Father, enters into the world's weakness and is generated in a new manner: invisible in his divine nature, he has become visible in ours.[124]

3.22 Even more significant for Christians than these conciliar documents themselves are the conclusions drawn from them and their interpretation or misinterpretation in catechetics, in preaching, in theology texts from the medieval summas to the modern manuals, and in popular piety. These conclusions, which are not necessarily a restatement of the conciliar positions, but in many respects represent a narrowing and hardening of these positions, can be summarized in two statements. First, the *person* of Jesus is divine and not human or, equivalently, in Jesus Christ there is no human person. Second, this divine person has at his disposal two ways of thinking, choosing and acting—a divine way and a human way.

3.3   The Heart of the Problem

If the conclusions alluded to in the last paragraph were correct *in the sense which we give to the word "person" today,* then Jesus would be nothing more than a mask or facade of God and the malaise spoken of at the beginning of this chapter would be more than justified. However, I believe that these conclusions are not correct and that they are little more than a thinly disguised docetism—the primordial heresy which sacrifices the real Jesus to an imagined "god," who has nothing whatsoever to do with the one whom Jesus himself called Father. Further, I believe that the conclusions above which claim to be drawn from conciliar teaching represent, precisely in their use of the word "person," a tragic misunderstanding of the New Testament data and a very unfortunate misinterpretation of the doctrine of the great councils, particularly of Chalcedon. Nevertheless, although these conclusions spoken of here are a patent distortion of the Jesus of the Gospels, I believe that the mistranslation of conciliar doctrine which is found in them is understandable and was to some degree even suggested by the conciliar documents themselves, because the councils were forced by the errors they were striving to combat to use a terminology which would prove to be dangerous in the extreme. Over and above this, behind the formal orthodoxy of the conciliar statements there may lurk, more often than not, Greek conceptions of the nature of God and man which are ill-suited to deal with the God who is the Father of Jesus Christ and with the human beings he came to save. These unfortunate effects of conciliar teaching could have been avoided if the councils were viewed not as independent sources of faith but rather as practical efforts of the Church at a particular moment in history to keep the scriptural message intact. But this was not the case and the councils were for all practical purposes regarded as sources of faith more important than Scripture itself. As a consequence, Christian faith has long been confronted with a variety of pseudo-problems, caused by the use of the word "person" in both trinitarian theology and Christology. If theology is to serve faith today, few questions are more important than that of *person* and *personality* in God and in Jesus Christ.

3.4 Person: An Introduction to the Discussion

No attempt will be made here to examine the modern notions of person and personality, as these concepts are used in fields as diverse as law, philosophy and psychoanalytic theory. What is worth attempting is a clear statement of what it means to talk about Jesus as a person and about God as a person. If the attempt is to succeed, three facts have to be taken account of: first, the word "person" has wide currency in ordinary speech, and in itself is not a technical term of either philosophy or theology; second, it is a word which points to the deeper levels of human experience, to the place where the human mystery resides; third, to talk about man and God as persons is to affirm that man achieves his identity, becomes a self, in dialogue with God, in hearing his word and speaking a word in return. These three facts suggest the proper procedure for understanding and using the word "person" in reference to God and Jesus: we can begin with a careful definition of the word as it is used in ordinary speech today, proceed by asking about the underlying mystery of personality which supports this ordinary usage, and finally ask how this underlying mystery of personality can be illuminated by the experience of man with God which is re- counted in the Old and New Testaments. (To propose such an approach to the problems raised by the concepts "person" and "personality" is, of course, to take a very definite position on the relationship of philosophy and theology. It is to assert that philosophy cannot make definitive statements about man and his situation because it is not an autonomous science. The factors which determine human existence are theological in the strict sense: they are constituted by and knowable through reve- lation—God's act of self-communication. Philosophy can pro- vide ways of reflecting on this act of God, and of expressing clearly and accurately both the knowledge of God we have attained and the limits of that knowledge.)

3.4 A survey of contemporary usage in regard to the word "person" indicates that apart from certain uses which could be classified as idiomatic or obsolescent[125] the word has three distinct but clearly interrelated meanings. It means the distinc- tive selfhood of the individual, the subject of rights and duties, and one who can meaningfully experience and influence the environment—abilities which are consequent on moral sense and consciousness. The first of these three meanings empha- sizes the uniqueness and incommunicability of the person; the second states, equivalently, that such a being is never a mere means but always an end in itself; the third strives to ground both the uniqueness and finality of the person in its relationship to intelligibility and value.

Popular usage of the term "person" already shows some effort to come to terms with its mystery, and I believe that it will not be difficult to penetrate to a deeper level and there to grasp the underlying structures and conditions of personhood. The method I propose to use is to begin with a global definition of person and then to analyze its elements and to clarify the meaning of the descriptive terms used. The global definition: a person is a being capable of understanding and love.

"Understanding" here is a synonym for intelligent knowledge. Such knowledge is not the registering or the categorizing of data or things. In essence it is not the fashioning of ideas of things or the making of mental images. It *is* the act of discovering, finding a value known as *reality* or *existence* in that which it has begun to experience in pre-intelligent forms of knowing. It is the act of holding concrete experience up in the light of our hunger for that which is not conditioned, not limited. It is the act which grasps the mystery of every finite thing because it respects the objective transcendence of the finite, that is, the implicit demand of finitude for transcendence, the demand of limited being to affirm it as embraced and supported by unlimited being. To call a person an intelligent knower is to see that every act in which we attain a limited truth is also an act in which we implicitly attain unlimited truth. To be an intelligent knower is to experience one's own being as the place where the world transcends itself, "takes one step beyond itself" in the direction of its infinite ground. To be a person is to experience infinity; to be a human person is to experience infinity as *gift*.

The type of knowledge which is described here has nothing to do with either confrontation or manipulation. It is not simply a condition for love; rightly understood, it already includes love. *Real* knowledge is always the act of welcoming the other (person or thing) into one's own self-awareness, the act of allowing the other to share in the transparency of one's own being and in its openness toward its infinite ground. Real knowledge for this reason is the act of including the other in one's own self-affirmation.

The second element of the mystery of the person is a

consequence of the fact that a person is an intelligent knower and lover; a person is a being who experiences life as a gift, both as a gift received and a gift to be given. To be a person is to perceive that life is preserved not by guarding it or securing it or immuring it in an impregnable citadel but rather by expending it on behalf of another. To be a person is to be aware of the great paradox that authentic life is life unsecured and life given. To be a person is to be the place where self-affirmation and affirmation of the other coincide.

The third element of the mystery of the person reflects the fact that to be a person is to willingly receive one's own being from another: a person is one who *speaks* a word to another and who asks that the word be heard and that a response be given. A person is one who *waits* for a word from another and who is willing to depend on this word. A person is one who knows that at the deepest level of his or her being he or she is the response to a call.

Is the notion of person which has been developed in the four paragraphs above applicable only to human persons, or can it be used of God as well? If this question means "Can the concept of human personality be extended, 'stretched,' so that it can include God?" then I believe the answer must be a firm *no*. The attempt to understand man and the world apart from God and then apply the concepts developed in this process to God will always fail, and it will always lead to unresolvable debates about a "personal" versus an "impersonal" God. On the other hand, if it is seen that to be a person is, essentially, *to be in dialogue*, then there is no question of applying a concept derived from the analysis of man to a heretofore unknown God; rather, the deepest mystery of the human person is seen to be constituted by the fact that the Infinite One has given himself, has spoken a word and waits for a response. God has taken to himself the willed vulnerability which is the heart of human personhood, and "person" is the only possible way of describing such a God.

Obviously, this brief summary could be expanded in many directions, but I believe that it will be most useful now to turn to the question of God and personality and to keep two questions in mind while doing this: "What does the New Testament say about the question (even though there is no single word for "person" in the New Testament text)?" and "What was the contribution of the early councils from Nicaea to Chalcedon?"

3.5 God and Personality

The word "God" in the New Testament means, almost without exception,[126] "the One Jesus called 'Father.' " This is by no means to assert that the New Testament takes no position on the question usually referred to as that of the divinity of Christ. But it is to assert that the statement "Jesus Christ is God" cannot be made as long as "God" is a word which refers to the one Jesus called "Father." For the remainder of this book, the content of this New Testament concept will be indicated in the following way: *God(nt)*. Now one thing is clear: *God(nt)* is *not* the one who Jesus is; he is rather the one whom Jesus faces, the one whose will he does, the one whose Son he is. The New Testament witness is constant and firm: *God(nt)* and Jesus are persons, distinct persons, different persons; and although the mystery of *God(nt)* clearly goes beyond that of human personality, it is just as clear that he possesses those characteristics which were identified in the preceding section as being constitutive of personality: he is one who knows and loves, he is the one who gives being and life, and he is the one who speaks a word of acceptance and waits for a response. *God(nt)* is clearly a person, and for the New Testament this is most evident in his dialogue with Jesus.

3.51 Jesus is clearly a person in the New Testament, but he is also a mysterious figure; he is close to *God(nt)*, and shares his life.[127] The various writings of the New Testament have different ways of speaking of this. Sometimes they talk of Jesus as "seated at the right hand of God"; at other times they call him the "Son of God" or "Word of God." In general, the New Testament refrains from calling Jesus *God* (remember that John 1:1 is speaking not precisely of Jesus but rather of the *Logos*). After about the year 150 A.D. it became common to explain the relationship of God and Jesus by *identifying* Jesus in some way with the Logos[128]—the word, thought, self-expression of *God(nt)*. Consequently, from this point on, a new question will become important: What is the relationship of the Logos to God? Nicaea will insist that the Logos has the *same underlying reality* as *God(nt)* and that he is "God of God."

3.52 This is a fateful moment, because now the word *God* ceases to designate solely the one Jesus calls "Father" and stops referring solely to the one *to whom* Jesus is related. At and after Nicaea, the word "God" no longer means *God(nt)*. It acquires a new and expanded meaning, a larger area of meaning: it comes to include both *God(nt)* and Jesus Christ, *as far as the latter is identified with the Logos.*[129] In this book this new concept of "God" will be indicated in the following way: *God(iv+)* (this is intended to show that this new concept of God was dominant from the fourth century on). From this moment on, it becomes possible, and sometimes necessary, to state that Jesus Christ is God, *provided one adopts the new linguistic convention of Nicaea and the later councils that the word "God" really means God(iv+).*

3.53 But at this juncture, something of crucial importance happened, to which theologians have not given nearly the attention which it deserves. When the term "God" acquired a new meaning and came to include both *God(nt)* and the Logos element in Jesus, *everything which was involved or implied in the personal relation-*

ship between Jesus and the Father in the New Testament is now assumed to exist "inside" God(iv+).[130] The word "God" no longer means "the person whose Son Jesus is." The new meaning *God(iv+)* includes Jesus and his Father, and therefore includes two who are *persons* in something very much like the modern sense of the word. Now it is clear that the New Testament sees Jesus and the Father as distinct persons: they have an "I-You" relationship; they are two "someones" who speak to each other and listen to each other. Each seems to have what we would call today a "distinct consciousness"; each has his own freedom, his own knowledge and his own love. Jesus and his Father exist in the greatest harmony, but they do so as *two persons* who are totally engaged in dialogue with each other. Jesus does the Father's will precisely because he makes the Father's will his own. He and the Father are "one" precisely as two who totally face each other.

3.54 As a result of projecting this personal distinction between Jesus and *God(nt)* into *God(iv+)*, that is, *into the divine life itself,* when a later theology will assert that there are three "persons" in God, *it will be tacitly assumed that there are distinct persons in God in the same sense in which Jesus and his Father are distinct and different persons in the New Testament.* It will be assumed that there are distinct "someones," each with his own consciousness, will, knowledge and freedom, who engage in dialogue with each other. Theological efforts to talk about the Trinity often start with this concept of person (distinctive consciousness, etc.— essentially the modern concept) and then proceed to "purify" the term by pointing out different elements of personality which cannot be found in *God(iv+)*. But at the end of this process, nothing remains of the concept of person as we use the word today, *except precisely that which is not true in God*—namely that there are distinct beings, each with his own consciousness, freedom, knowledge and will.

3.55 But can this be said, that there is no multiplicity of persons in this sense of the word in God? Not only *can* this be said, but it *must* be, if we want to remain true not only to the evidence of the New Testament but also to the constant teaching of the Church since the time of the great christological councils of the fourth and fifth centuries. The teaching of the Church on this question has been constant and uniform: in God there is only one knowledge, one love, one consciousness and one freedom.[131] This is equivalent to saying that in God there are no persons *in our sense of the word*—that is, beings capable of engaging in dialogue with each other precisely because each has his or her distinct consciousness and freedom. The second "person" of the Trinity is the word which the Father speaks, and is not to be thought of as turning around and "speaking back" to the Father, any more than our words speak back to us. The third "person" of the Trinity is the gift which is given, and it does not turn around and "give itself back" to the Father and the Son (except in pious trinitarian speculation which has no basis either in the New Testament or in the official teaching of the Church).

To call Jesus the "Word" or the "Son" does not imply that Jesus was present in heaven, before the incarnation, conversing with the Father and the Spirit as a distinct person, who would later, *as this same person,* take a human nature as his own, and discharge for this nature those functions usually discharged by a human personality.[132] When the New Testament presents Jesus as engaging in dialogue with his Father, this should not be thought of as the continuation of a conversation which began in eternity. Jesus is the first to speak to *God(nt)* as his *Son,* and when he does, *God(nt)* who exists from all eternity as the infinite Mystery, the One with no beginning or origin, *becomes definitively and irrevocably Father.* Jesus Christ is *God's(nt)* Son because he is the fulfillment in history of *God's(nt)* eternal decision not to remain silent, not to remain alone. If *God(nt)* had simply called into being the things which are not, he would have been Creator; but he has done much more. He has willed to come, himself, into the alien domain of non-being. His is the mystery of the infinite one who has willed to exist in finitude; his is the mystery of the perfect being who has willed to share the broken being of the world, to make this broken being his very own, and in that act to take it into the healing mystery of his own life.

3.56 Even before the birth of Jesus and before the creation of the world, there is a distinction within the divine life, within the infinite being of God, between his being in and for himself and his being able to be the exemplar of all creation. This could be thought of as a distinction beteen God as *origin* and God as *Word,* and it is real in eternity. Otherwise, God would not be able to share *himself* with his creatures, would not be able to be *Father* to his human creatures, but would, at best, remain a distant prime mover or first cause. The real distinction within the divine life is the ground and basis of the self-sharing which becomes definitive and irrevocable in Jesus Christ. This is what it means to speak of the distinction of *hypostaseis* in God from eternity, and *it is within this framework that the question of the pre-existence of the Logos must be discussed.* But note: this distinction which must be affirmed as real in *God(nt)* is *not* a distinction of persons in the only sense in which we can use that word today. In *our* sense of the word *person,* Jesus and his Father are personally distinct; Father and Logos are not. There is nothing in Scripture and nothing in the formal statements of the councils which implies that the distinction of *hypostaseis* within God has anything to do with our understanding of the word *person* today (although it should be recognized that the Latin word *persona* was already ambiguous and could lead to a mythologizing of the distinctions within God, as can be seen in Leo's letter to Flavian, shortly before the Council of Chalcedon).[133]

3.6 Crypto-Tritheism and Modern Atheism

The notion that there are three persons in God, in the sense in which we inevitably understand the word *person* today, is not an assertion of faith; it is a denial of the real God, because it is the refusal to allow Jesus to be the one who defines *God(nt)* and the refusal to allow *God(nt)* to be the one who defines himself and determines the one he will be, in Jesus. The only real God is the one who defines himself in Jesus, but man rejected this God then and continues to reject him down through history. Man fashions his own "god"—unreal in itself, but real enough as a projection of his own desire to manipulate and to control, his own desire to evade the responsibility proper to an historical being whose task is to create the future. This "god" we create has many faces, but in terms of the present problem, he could be described this way: he is supreme and perfect, eternal and immutable. Since before the beginning he has possessed all possible perfection, all of the values which might ever be attained in history, even if it were to run its course thousands of times. Such a "god" might be called personal, and it might even be asserted that personal dialogue takes place within such a "god." Even so, such a "god" is a threat to the dignity of life and the seriousness of history. Such a "god"is the one rejected by much serious modern atheism. But such a "god" never existed anyway.

The root error here is that this "god" we fashion is, himself, above and beyond history. He may *appear* in history, but history remains a stage on which he might walk, so that people could view him, and perhaps perceive a little of the perfection which he had before history began and which he would have had even if there had been no history. Such a "god" has no history and cannot take history seriously. If we succeed in installing this "god" in high heaven, we have no history either and we do not have to take seriously the task of creating the future and of being responsible for the world. Such a "god" can be served and placated by the performance of specifically "religious" duties; he lays claim only to a sector of our lives—the sacred—and leaves the rest of the world to us. Small wonder that we are tempted to invent him and then to bow down before the idol which is the work of our own hands.

3.7 The Real God

But *God(nt)* is different. His engagement on behalf of the world and on our behalf is identical with his own being and his own life. His own life is not definitively real aside from us or apart from us, *because this is the way he wanted it to be.* God does not reveal himself by remaining in eternity and making copies or replicas of himself which he then inserts into time. Rather, God reveals himself by *being here.* He does not keep himself above the world, untouched by it. His own being is the ground of possibility from all eternity for his engagement with the world, and distinct from this, within his own being, is his decision to have Jesus for a Son and to intend all that this decision implies, from the first atom to the farthest star, from the earliest forms of primitive life to the last example of *homo futurus.*

This real God is very different from the idol which we fashion in our own image and likeness, and he could be described this way: *God(nt)* is one who shares his being with us. He exists precisely in doing this, and from all eternity he is the one who willed to *be himself* in time and in history. What he willed to be from "before" the beginning, he *is,* definitively and irrevocably only in Jesus—namely the *Father,* our Father. He becomes the one he eternally chose to be in and through his presence in Christ, reconciling the world to himself.

Some might be interested in speculating on the possibility of God's being other than he is (namely, the one committed to us). It is difficult to evaluate such speculation, because the only

God(nt) there is or ever has been is so committed to Jesus, to us
and to our history that this history has become his very own.
Jesus' history is God's own, and therefore if Christ is one of us
and if, in some sense, we share the same being, type of existence, then our history does not take place outside the life of
God. The call of Jesus is not to rise above history, to leave the
world behind, so that we might encounter God in the timeless
sameness of eternity. In and through Jesus, our history becomes
God's history and our decisions become absolutely important.
In the fullest sense of the word, Jesus offers us a history because
he makes the real future possible—a future which is not in any
sense "there" (even in the mind of God) before we create it. It is
this which gives meaning to our decisions and which confers
dignity on human life. To have a history is to be one who
becomes a self through one's own choice and decision.

Because God is so thoroughly committed to Jesus, it becomes important to ask whether this history goes on after the
death of Jesus. That it does is the meaning of the resurrection.
In and through Jesus' death, God became so completely and
exhaustively *for us* that his history became our history. In Jesus,
God(nt) remains in history, and the historical destiny of all human beings is determined by their stance toward Jesus. Those
who have no knowledge of Jesus at all have no history. Those
who know Jesus only anonymously have only a germinal, incipi-
ent history. Those who know and accept him as the Son of
God(nt) enjoy true freedom and have the power to create an
authentic future.

3.8 Summary

We have no access to *God(nt)* other than through Jesus
Christ, and the only valid statements about God are those which
are derived from the word and work of Jesus. The life of the
triune God in himself is not to be, and cannot be, distinguished

from his life as lived for us. *God(nt)* is the eternal commitment to Jesus, and because of this there is a distinction, eternally, in the divine life, between God as ground and God as imitable—that is, God as Logos or Word. This distinction is not there "for God's good" but for ours. God's eternal decision to share his own being is his eternal commitment to Jesus, and because God always wanted to be this way, there is an eternal differentiation in the divine life itself. Jesus is "what happened" because God decided not simply to create historical beings but to become a participant in history. The Logos or Word of God is the ground of possibility for this event, the reason it *could* happen. The human being, Jesus (and in our sense of the word the human *person*), is conclusive evidence that it *did* happen. Jesus is the result of God's decision to love personally—to offer personal love and to await a commensurate response. All that came before Jesus was God's preparation for the one who would call him "Father." The Trinity is not "God in himself," as though he could be thought of apart from human destiny. The Trinity is the only God there is—that is, *God for us.* Christ's humanity is not the vesture of *God(nt).* If we want to use the word "humanity" or "human nature" at all, the terms simply mean "the way this human person Jesus can and does act"—this human person who, precisely as such, is the word, the presence, the reality of *God(nt)* among us.

3.9 Final Note on the Word "God"

There is one obvious question which this chapter cannot evade: What judgment should be passed on Nicaea's redefinition of the word "God"? I believe that the judgment will have to be a nuanced one, and that it contains three elements, which suggests that we should at least think about the possibility of returning to the earlier linguistic convention on the word "God."

3.91 It should be admitted that Nicaea's redefinition was *inevitable.* John's Gospel itself provided later theology with the category of *Logos* or *Word* for interpreting the relationship between Jesus and *God(nt).* This was developed by the apologists, and by the early third century it had become a commonplace to identify the Logos with some *central element* in Jesus Christ. Early in this tradition, it was commonly said that the Logos was "in" Jesus; later it became more common to say that the Logos *was* Jesus, in the sense of being identified with *the one who Jesus was.*

A second fact which made Nicaea's redefinition inevitable was the Greek notion that God in himself can have no direct contact with creation, and that his creative will and act must be *mediated* by one who is not identified *totally* with God. *Logos* served this function, and within Arianism it was precisely the distinction between Logos and God that made creation a possibility.

This typically Greek notion of Logos was inherently unstable. If it emphasized the distinction between the Logos and God, it went the way of Arianism. On the other hand, if, in full acceptance of the Old Testament revelation, it affirmed that the real God is both self-sufficient *and* really engaged in the world on our behalf, it had to affirm the divinity of the Logos: the fact that the Logos is God.

3.92 Given the resources of thought and expression which were available to the Church in Nicaea's time, the redefinition of the word "God" was *necessary.* The New Testament evidence is clear on this point: in Jesus, no one other than God *himself* is engaged; Jesus is something other than a mere creature: he lives, precisely as this human person, the very life of God. The only means available to theology at the time which could state this clearly was the concept of *physis* or *ousia,* and therefore it was necessary to state that Jesus has the same *underlying reality* as God. But since the underlying reality is that which makes God divine, makes God himself, makes him God, Nicaea has to say that the Logos *is* God.

3.93 But a third point is equally important: there is dangerous *ambiguity* in calling Jesus or the Logos *God.* The word "is" when used of God means two things: first, it means his *eternal self-sufficient act of existence;* second, it means his *commitment to time and history* as the Father of Jesus. The mystery of God is the mystery of the identity amid distinction of these acts of existence. But the Greek mind is incapable of understanding God's existence as essentially committed to time, space and history, and to call Jesus or the Logos *God* is, for the Greek mind, tantamount to placing the personal dialogue between Jesus and the Father within the eternal life of God. This misses the real uniqueness of Jesus and places an insuperable obstacle in the way of taking his humanity seriously. When God's historical engagement in Jesus is transferred to the plane of eternity, before history began, the essential mystery of Jesus is beyond recovery. In reality, Jesus is our only access to *God(nt).* "God" is not a title which Jesus came to claim. He came to define the word "God" and to proclaim the good news that the "god" who men thought existed in reality did not. Jesus did not seek to be called "God," and it is a dubiously Christian endeavor to insist on calling him that to-day—not because it says too much but because it says far too little.

3.94 What would happen if we returned to the linguistic convention of the New Testament and used the word "God" to refer only to *God(nt)*—that is, to the one whom Jesus called "Father"? Certainly it would be no infringement on the integrity of faith, because it would be difficult to argue that faith in New Testament times was less vital and authentic than it is today. On the other hand, there would seem to be many advantages. The danger of fashioning a remote, immutable, tri-personal "god" would be far less, because the dialogue between Jesus and his Father would not be forced out of history into eternity. Most important of all, the way would be cleared for a new understanding of the relation between the human and the divine, not only in Jesus, but in all of creation. More than any other factor, the Nicene redefinition of the word "God" has been responsible for an understanding of humanity and divinity which sees them as essentially *competitive*—as though Jesus became "more divine" if we make him less human, and as though God is in competition with other human beings for our attention, loyalty and love.

The effects of this essentially competitive Christology on dogma and on Christian decision-making have been destructive in the extreme, and it is tempting to think of what the effects on faith and life might be if Jesus were seen to be the one in whom humanity and human personality became *sacraments* of the presence of *God(nt)*. In such a view, it is precisely in affirming that Jesus is exhaustively and totally human that we would come on his mystery and on the very mystery of God. It would then be seen that humanity and divinity in Christ and in the rest of creation do not stand in a relation of inverse proportion (as one increases the other decreases) but rather in a relation of direct proportion—in affirming the humanity of Christ, we would finally come to understand the mystery of his union with God, because we would finally come to understand who God is. But can we go back to the linguistic conventions of the New Testament, now that sixteen hundred years have passed since Nicaea's fateful step? I will return to this question, at least indirectly, in the next chapter.

The Problem of
Jesus Today

4.1 The Problem of Speculative Christology

Speculative Christology is nothing more than the attempt to understand Jesus Christ as one who has a unique relationship with God and with us, his fellow human beings. Here, different approaches are possible, and, in fact, different ways have been taken by theology in the past. Up until the very recent past, it was tacitly assumed that the great christological councils of the early Church (Nicaea to Chalcedon) had said the definitive word on the mystery of Jesus Christ and that the task of speculative Christology today was simply to "redo" this conciliar theology with the help of words and concepts which had been refined in the work of theologians since 451 A.D. The theologians on whose work the greatest reliance was placed were the "Scholastics"—the authors of the great medieval *Summas,* or summaries of theology. Among these various *Summas,* that of Thomas Aquinas, the *Summa Theologiae,* held the place of honor since the middle of the fourteenth century and had been given official status, both in respect to content and method, by Leo XIII in 1879. The period of the great medieval Scholastics was followed by a period of their great commentators, down to about the time of the Reformation. After the Reformation this tradition had gone into decline, and until well into the nineteenth century, "Thomists" and other representatives of this late Scholasticism showed little vitality and less ability to adapt their masters' thought to contemporary problems.[134] It was the encyclical letter of Leo XIII, alluded to above,[135] which revived the thought of Thomas Aquinas in the years after 1879 and which inspired the rather impressive attempt to grapple with present-day problems on the basis of this thirteenth century corpus of theology. This neo-Scholasticism or neo-Thomism, as it was called, was an attempt at restoration, and like all such attempts, it was destined to fail. Like neo-Romanesque and neo-Gothic architecture, neo-Scholastic thought was not without a certain brilliance in the hands of its most gifted practitioners, but its loyalty was really to the past and it was unwilling to take seriously the epoch-making developments in man's self-understanding which had taken place in the six centuries since the death of Thomas Aquinas.

However, with very few exceptions, neo-Scholasticism was the way Catholic theology was done almost up to the time of the Second Vatican Council. For two reasons this fact encouraged the view that the task of Christology was to explain and defend the decrees of the great christological councils of the early Church. First, Thomas himself took the ecclesiastical tradition embodied in these councils as a *source* of theology; second, Thomas and the other Scholastics were intent on using the resources of Greek thought to understand Christian doctrine and therefore they found the work of the early councils very congenial.

Because Scholasticism and neo-Scholasticism have determined both the method and the content of Christology up until very recently, it will be a good thing to comment briefly here on the collapse of the neo-Scholastic synthesis and to assess both the dangers and the possibilities inherent in this event.

4.2   Neo-Scholasticism and Christology

The collapse of the neo-Scholastic synthesis in the past two decades has marked an important turning point for Catholic theology in general and for Christology in particular. The syn-

thesis itself was a product of three factors which are best described as styles of thinking. The first was neo-Scholastic
philosophy itself, abstracted not (as most of its practitioners
believed) from the theological writings of Thomas Aquinas, but
resting in the main on the interpretations of commentators from
Giles of Rome down to Etienne Gilson and Jacques Maritain.
The second constitutive element of the neo-Scholastic synthesis
was a particular view of the teaching authority of the Church
which did not see in this office or function the task of interpreting Scripture, but wanted it, instead, to play the role of a *source*
of faith and theology (and, in practice if not in theory, the
principal source). This particular view had developed rapidly
since 1870 (the date of the First Vatican Council) and had been
stated with all desirable clarity by Pius XII in his encyclical letter
of 1950, *Humani Generis.*[136] The third element of the neo-Scholastic synthesis was its concept or definition of theology: it saw
theology as a technique of deriving conclusions ("theses") of
different degrees of certitude by applying formal logic to prem-
ises or statements proposed by the teaching authority of the
Church.

The neo-Scholastic synthesis collapsed not because Thomas Aquinas or the teaching authority of the Church or formal
logic has been discredited, individually or collectively (although
some have rather naively suggested just this), but because a
more careful look at the three styles of thinking alluded to above
led to the suspicion that the neo-Scholastic system was misinter-
preting Thomas, miscasting the teaching authority of the
Church and misunderstanding the nature of theology. The old
synthesis collapsed not because a more successful competitor
had replaced it but simply because its own foundations were
weak. However, system and synthesis are not a luxury: they
provide both structure and direction for thought, without which
the theological enterprise will dissipate its energies in aimless
theorizing.

The collapse of the old synthesis resulted in a failure of nerve among many who had been trained in Thomism and conditioned to unquestioning acceptance of that considerable body of papal literature which had been produced between the two Vatican Councils. It was inevitable that this failure of nerve would have serious consequences for the Church, for theology is not an intellectual pastime for religious dilettantes but an essential function of Church life, and the Church is poorly served by a theology which is plagued by doubts about its real relevance to the human situation. And precisely this seems to be the problem of much contemporary Catholic theology: it has lost its sense of identity, its grasp of where it stands among the other disciplines. In recent years, it has been common to confuse concern for the human situation with total absorption in it. In fact, a surprising number of theologians have apparently felt that their task was to theorize about the escapades of political and social activists, and many came to share the latter's contempt of a stable order which draws on the resources of the past. This type of anti-intellectualism is destructive of theology; under its sway theology becomes so completely immersed in the changing situation and its ephemeral fashions that it loses the power to address that situation, to criticize it and to judge it. The Church will survive the collapse of the neo-Scholastic system—it has faced far greater crises—but if Catholic theology is to derive any benefit from the event it will have to come to a clearer understanding of its task. There is only one foundation on which a new synthesis can be built and only one center from which the work of reconstructing Catholic theology can proceed: a critical assessment of the primary source of all Christian faith and life, the New Testament itself. It is theology's task to understand and articulate *this* message, in the conviction that if it is clearly heard it will show itself to be a word of power. Above all, a sound systematic Christology can be constructed only by returning to this document, in which the word of Jesus and the word about him reached a form in which they would be accessible to later generations and in which they could continue to play a critical role in the life of the Church and of the individual Christian.

4.3   Christology and the New Testament

Even when it is clearly seen that the task of Christology is to understand the Jesus of the New Testament and not to dissect the Christ of the councils with ever greater subtlety, different approaches are possible. But here the question is largely that of how much space and time should be given to the exegesis of the Gospels—that is, to the understanding and interpretation of the text itself. A detailed exegesis of even one of the Gospels would exceed the limits of space and time which are proper to this book; furthermore, there are books available which contain excellent summaries of modern critical study of the Gospels.[137] However, it is not only disappointing to be referred to some fine work which one does not have at hand; here it would not be appropriate because of certain specific questions which systematic Christology *must* bring to the study of the Gospels. There is no question here of forcing the Gospels to answer modern questions in modern terms, but it is legitimate to ask if the Gospels might not have some very good answers to our questions if we have the patience to listen and to translate the answers the Gospels give into the totally different language we speak today.[138] As we search for Jesus today we can't really ignore the sixteen centuries of theological discussion about his underlying reality, the distinction of principles of operation in him, and his own subjectivity and most profound identity. Jesus today bears this burden—one which he did not have to bear in his own day—and it is the task of a good systematic Christology to lift this burden from him. If we are going to discharge this task properly, we will have to ask questions about *ousia* and *physis* and *hypostasis* in Jesus, about his *natura* and *persona;* but most of all we will have to ask if our modern terms *nature* and *person* do justice to his mystery, and, if so, in precisely what sense. It is inevitable that we approach the Gospels with certain questions in mind and we are right in expecting the Gospels to give an answer—although sometimes the answer may be unexpected and may suggest that our questions themselves are couched in misleading terms.

4.31   For these reasons I will not presume that the reader has a thorough acquaintance with modern critical work on the Gospels, nor will I try to summarize that work precisely as it bears on the historical Jesus.[139] Rather, I will present a relatively brief picture of Jesus which is based on the best contemporary exegesis but which concentrates on the question of his identity, and therefore on the problem of his mysterious relationship with the one he called "God" or "Father" and on the problem of his authentic membership in the human race.

In the final analysis, speculative Christology exists to help us meet Jesus. It is not justified by the subtlety of its speculation or by its success in "proving" the truth; it is justified only by its success in mediating the encounter with him. Since one of the privileged forms of the presence of Jesus today is in his *word,* in the proclamation recorded in the New Testament, one of the main tasks of Christology will be to remove obstacles to the encounter with Jesus in the New Testament word, so that this word may become transparent to *him,* to this man who remains the ground and basis of our faith. But note carefully: Christology is important precisely because it can mediate the encounter with *him, in his word in the New Testament.* No summary of Jesus' word and work can succeed if it tries to condense him and his message into a few (or very many) general truths, which we could then reflect on independently of him. The message which Jesus preached and the message which he was and is can never be effective as a body of truths *about which* we might think and *therefore from which we might distance ourselves.* There is something peculiar about Jesus' word which distinguishes it from the words of others, whether philosophers or religious founders, and which has much to do with the mystery of Jesus himself: his word is effective only when it remains *his* word, the word of a *living person,* which I experience as addressed to me. In this situation I know that I am called by one who lives, to be an attentive and obedient listener; I may accept or reject this word, but I can no more distance myself from this word than I can from my very self.

The summary of the meaning and mystery of Jesus which I attempt in the next few pages would be pointless if it were an attempt to formulate even a very good set of moral and dogmatic theses about Jesus which then made the encounter with his living word unnecessary. But there is a point to what follows: as we strive to hear the word of the Lord, we can reflect on what we begin to hear, so that we may hear it more attentively. Hopefully, now that we have seen some of the limits and dangers of an overly literal repetition of conciliar theology, we will be able to hear the word of Jesus and the word about him more clearly, so that we may encounter *him* and not the artificial being constructed by Scholastic thought on the basis of a conciliar terminology which is largely unintelligible today.

4.4   Jesus of Nazareth: His Claim, His Message, His Mystery

Early in this century Albert Schweitzer wrote a now classic work in which he documented the failure of theologians in the nineteenth century to write a convincing life of Jesus. He pointed out that all of them set out resolutely to find the Jesus they wanted and needed—a Jesus who was, in the final analysis, a good nineteenth century liberal—and therefore their attempts had to fail, because the Jesus whom the nineteenth century dreamed of never existed. Schweitzer was convinced that the

real Jesus would have been incomprehensible to that century
and would have been perceived as a strange and alien being.
Toward the end of the same book, Schweitzer sketched a picture
of Jesus which attempted to show that the man from Nazareth
was no less a stranger to his own age. Schweitzer's Jesus was a
man of strange and dark imaginings, obsessed with the thought
that the end of the world was imminent—a man who threw
himself on the wheel of history to force it to a stop, but who,
instead, was broken by the wheel and died a failure.[140]

Historical-critical study of the Gospels was scarcely out of
its infancy in Schweitzer's day. Today, although no reputable
scholar would dream of writing a biography of Jesus, a broad
and solid consensus can be found among exegetes, in respect to
the fundamental meaning of Jesus and of his message.[141]
Schweitzer's own picture of the historical Jesus has not stood the
test of time and of critical scholarship in any of its details, but it
is clear that in one respect he was right: Jesus is not only a
stranger in our world; he was, if anything, even more a stranger
in his own. In their own way, the Gospel writers were as much at
a loss in grappling with the strangeness and otherness of Jesus
as were the liberal theologians who attempted those nineteenth
century "lives of Jesus." It is by examining their efforts to fit
Jesus into their own world and into its categories of thought and
action, and *above all in examining the failure of these efforts,* that we
can come to understand Jesus today.[142]

4.41   The New Testament writers give us many different pictures of Jesus: exorcist, miracle-worker, rabbi, Messiah, Lord,
Son of Man and Son of God. These are only a few of the images
which the Jewish world of his own day offered (many of them
with deep and ancient roots in Jewish and Israelite history).
Before the development of critical methods for reading the New
Testament, the Gospels were often read in order to find evidence for these titles (or in order to confirm what one already

"knew" about him from other sources). These "other sources" which provided the truths about Jesus that could be proved or confirmed by the New Testament were, of course, the teachings of the various Christian Churches—teachings which themselves had often originated centuries before anyone asked if the failure of the Gospel writers to understand Jesus might not be just as revelatory as their success.

As a result, the New Testament and the teaching of the various Churches seemed to reinforce each other, particularly in regard to the *titles* of Jesus—Messiah, Son of God, God—and in regard to his functions, or "offices" as they were called, of *prophet, priest* and *king.* Much of what passed for New Testament theology in the pre-critical age consisted in the attempt to determine the meaning of these various titles and offices, and then to prove that they were rightly applied to Jesus or even that he claimed them—particularly the titles of *Messiah* and *God.*

4.42 Today I believe it is safe to say that the real mystery of Jesus is manifest in the fact that he was very much a stranger in his world. The attempts of people who knew him and of those who wrote shortly after his time to classify or categorize him were not very successful. Mark's Gospel, the first to be written, preserves more stories which show this than do the later Gospels. For Mark, misunderstanding dogs Jesus' steps—his family, his followers, his most intimate associates fail to grasp the meaning of his words and acts.[143] There is something strangely *elusive* about him. Luke's account of how the people in Nazareth wanted to put him to death by throwing him over a cliff is certainly apocryphal, but there is something symbolic about the end of the story: "He slipped through their hands." They thought they held him, but suddenly he was not there. He did that in his own day and he has been doing it ever since.

This is obviously true of the more far-fetched attempts to present Jesus in a way which might make him attractive or intelligible to our day and age. (As fads come and go the attempts have to be updated with embarrassing frequency.) In the mid-1960's more than one attempt was made to show that Jesus was really a political and social activist—perhaps even an early representative of the "theology" of revolution. Such efforts are rather transparent surveys of what one or another author wishes Jesus had said or done, because they must begin by ignoring the fact that Jesus evidently took no position in regard to the brutal occupation of his country by a foreign power or in respect to social evils such as slavery and the systematic oppression of the poor. Far from calling for efforts to alleviate the tragic situation of the poor, he dares to call them "happy" and to suggest that in some way the meaning of God's rule is accessible to them. Any social romanticism in regard to the poor is notably absent from the earliest "Jesus material"[144] and from those sayings which have the strongest title to authenticity.

But even the more traditional ways of understanding Jesus do not do justice to him. It would seem safe to call him the founder of the Christian religion, but again the earliest traditions show that he was quite dubious about the whole enterprise of religion. It is not simply that he criticized abuses—the rabbis before and after him had done that and would do it again. It is rather that he seems to regard the very attempt of man to arrange his relationship with God through religious practice as futile and, ultimately, as an act of disloyalty to God.

For centuries Christians were impressed by the miracles which Jesus had worked, according to the Gospel tradition, and it is clear that for Mark something essential about Jesus was revealed in the *exorcisms*. But here, too, there are serious problems. It is not simply that the Synoptic miracle tradition is no longer regarded as historical by critical (and *Christian*) scholarship today. Even more than this, there are traces of Jesus' own reserve in respect to attempts to reduce him to the level of a wonder-worker, and some unwillingness on his part to be "typed" this way must stand behind the so-called messianic secret, as we find it in Mark and to a lesser degree in Matthew and Luke. In any case, Jesus never seems to have seen the healings as proofs of his divinity or of any other claims he made.

He must have impressed many in his day as a wandering religious teacher, and the title "teacher" or "rabbi" which we find often enough on the lips of his followers may well be historical. But the term meant, in his day, *teacher of the law,* and this he emphatically was not. No rabbi would dare deal with the law in the sovereign fashion in which he did. No rabbi would have associated with the ritually unclean and the sinners as he did. And no rabbi would have been described as a glutton and a drunkard (a story which his followers would not have passed on unless the accusation had really been made). Jesus was no moral teacher—he seems indifferent to general norms of moral activity and he has nothing to do with casuistry. Any attempt to write a good moral theology today on the basis of the general principles which Jesus taught will be a failure.[145]

Efforts to present Jesus as prophet, priest and king really derive from an over-literal reading of certain New Testament writings. The Epistle to the Hebrews is invoked for the title "priest" and John's Gospel for the title "king." The early Church may have toyed with the possibility of presenting Jesus as prophet because of Jewish expectations at the time, but there is no evidence that Jesus saw himself in this light. In fact, the term "prophet" as it was defined in the Old Testament is peculiarly inappropriate as a description of his work. Jesus resembles the prophets in some ways; like them he speaks the word of Yahweh to the contemporary world. But in a most important respect Jesus differs from the prophets: they experienced the word of God as something profoundly *alien* which was imposed upon them almost against their will. It was a word which they had to speak but a word which often enough they did not want to speak. They were spokesmen for God, yet the burden of speaking his word was one from which they would gladly be free. But Jesus speaks the word of God as though it is, at the same time, *his own word.* Without giving any justification, he acts as though the forgiveness which he offers is God's own,[146] and he implies that nothing less than the rule of God is manifest in his words and acts.[147] Jesus never "disappears" behind his word: his word (which is also God's word) is very much a projection or extension of himself.

4.43   The word "Messiah" holds a special place among all the titles of Jesus. In the early days of the Church it was so favored that in its Greek translation—Christos—it practically became Jesus' second name, and in more modern times Jesus' alleged claim to the title has been one of the principal ways of proving his divinity. A careful critical study of the Gospels indicates that with high probability Jesus never used the term of himself and that its use about him by others during his lifetime is very unlikely.[148] More fruitful than the discussion of these various probabilities is the text of Mark 8:29ff where Jesus asks Peter's view of who he (Jesus) is. According to Mark, Peter responds with the confession that Jesus is the Messiah. Rather than accepting this title and praising Peter (as he does in Matthew's text), Jesus reacts by telling his followers not to let anyone in on the secret and then proceeds to *redefine* the title in a way which would have made it unrecognizable to any Jew from the time of David down to his own day (that is, he redefined it in terms of suffering).[149]

The word "redefine" is a useful one here; every term, every title has to be redefined before it can apply to him. There is no description of him and his work that can really "hold" him. He is, in this respect, strangely elusive, and something very essential about his mystery comes to light here. All of the titles we

have examined briefly here try to specify who he is in relation to
the God of his people, but there is something about him which
escapes this specification, and this is a most important fact. He can't
be defined, and the reason seems to be that he brings something
so radically new and different into the world that all of the old
categories for specifying the relationship of man and God are
simply inadequate to the task of describing him. All of this
suggests that he cannot be defined in relation to God *precisely
because he is the one who defines what the word "God" means.*

4.44 Jesus' relationship with God is mysterious and absolutely
unique, and the only way to describe it is to talk of it as *immediate*
in the literal sense of this word: there is no one and nothing
between him and God, and there are many things that he says
and does which make this immediacy clear.

   Jesus is one who talks and teaches with *authority.*[150] His
words have a convincing power that comes to people as a
surprise; their religious leaders usually do not teach this way.
They are content to comment on the law and to repeat the
teaching of the ancients, but he brings a new[151] teaching that no
one has heard before. This teaching is not just something that
he does; he seems to regard the proclamation of this teaching as
his essential task.

   This teaching is radically new, and, in fact, it relativizes the
whole religious tradition of his people. More than anything else
this is an indication of his closeness to God: in the name of the
God with whom he is on intimate terms he sets the law aside.
His attitude toward fasting, toward the observance of the sab-
bath and toward ritual washing cannot be interpreted in any
other way,[152] and in the story recounted in Mark 7:1–23 he calls
into question the basic presupposition of all ancient (and modern!) religiosity.[153] Those theologians of the Bultmann school
who have given us the "new quest of the historical Jesus" have
rightly emphasized the importance of the antitheses in Matthew

5:21ff: Jesus lays claim to his hearers with a totality which not only goes beyond the law of Moses; his claim is really in conflict with the law of Moses and with the fundamental assumptions which stand behind this law. He simply sets the law aside, and the religious leadership of his people must be credited with seeing this more clearly than many Christians have.

Jesus is not given to making statements of principle about the special privileges of Israel and about the Jewish people's unique place in the plan of God, but on more than one occasion he suggested that however real these privileges, they might be set aside. The implication is that he knows who God is and what God wants, while those who rely on religious tradition do not have this knowledge.[154] He is remarkably cavalier about deporting himself in a "religious" way: the little story of Mark 7:24–30 is a gem in this respect. He is outside the Holy Land and talking with a pagan (apparently a woman from one of the Phoenician cities). She talks to Jesus in a rather flip way, and he seems to like this and enjoy it—in fact, he seems to act as though her distinctly unreligious conduct is really an act of faith.

Again and again, Jesus seems to want to make the point that there are no pre-conditions which have to be met in order to secure the mercy of God. God *is* merciful, in and of himself, and salvation is not something to be won or merited; it is a gift. When Jesus remarks that God can do anything, the context of the statement is not really that of God's power, but that of God's *mercy:* God is so powerful that he can even get the rich into heaven![155] What we are all called upon to do is to accept just that—to be like children, who can accept a gift without calculating how and when it is to be paid back.[156] By the same token, of course, no one can have any claim on God. (Paul gives us almost no information about the historical Jesus, but his doctrine of the "justification" which the sinner receives from God purely as a gift is an accurate interpretation of Jesus' own teaching, particularly as we find the latter in Mark's Gospel. This fact is even more striking because the terminology is entirely different.)

Jesus' attitude toward religion is, to put it mildly, *distanced.* The people who follow him and who feel at ease in his company are a peculiar group, and there is really only one thing they have in common: the absence of any natural or acquired aptitude for understanding his message or for being of much use in the establishment of the kingdom. Certainly, no rabbi or scribe would have wanted anything to do with them, but he did: he simply reached into the lives of very unlikely people and told them to follow him, and they did.

Jesus did all of this in the name of the real God and he did it with supreme confidence. When a paralyzed man came looking for a cure (Mk 2:1–11) Jesus told him that his sins were forgiven—that is, that what had separated him from God was over and done with. (The story as we now have it has undoubtedly been modified. Mark himself may have joined it to a story about a healing, and the stitches still show. But the real point of the original story remains and the scribes present see it immediately: only God can forgive sins, and this man is acting in the name of God, without giving any justification and without asking for the approval of the religious leaders of his people.)

Jesus acts as though a decisive change in world history has occurred with his arrival on the scene: something definitive and final has happened and the good news is there for the taking. God is in charge, and this means that the time of peace, joy, justice and life has come for everyone. Furthermore, this good news is not just something that Jesus talks about; he brings this new time of peace, and in some way it is *identified* with him. *He does not inaugurate a new religious tradition* but rather brings God to his hearers in the world where they are, at the same time *laying claim to them in all of their worldly existence.* The gift which he offers is total, but so is the demand which he makes. He will not be satisfied with mere religious performance or with merely religious conversion. The good news which he brings is so good that he wants people to rely on it, to base their lives on it, and to turn away from everything else. In the name of this good news, he confidently overturns accepted values, not only in the religious sphere but everywhere in life. From now on, success and failure will have different meanings and all of the standards of the world will be relativized. (This is the meaning of the saying about the losing and the gaining of life which we find in Mark 8:34–38.) Jesus is absolutely certain that God is behind the good news which he brings, and that no matter how insignificant it may appear in the beginning, in the end it will win through because the power of God is with it. (All of the parables of the kingdom seem to be making this point; it is particularly clear in Mark 4:1–9, although the verses which follow, up to verse 20, show that the point may have been missed even before Mark's time. They also show how strong the tendency was to make Jesus into a moralist and a religious founder.)[157]

It is the unheard of *totality* of Jesus' claim which indicates how confident he was of speaking in God's name. The so-called Beatitudes are an outstanding example of this attitude of his; no subtle casuistry can find any loopholes there, but for this very reason, these sayings of his cannot be interpreted as law. Love cannot be commanded, but by the same token the directive to love one's neighbor *as oneself* (with all of the implications of clever planning and untiring dedication!) cannot be evaded. Here, as always, Jesus never really talks *about* God. He confronts his hearers with God's own challenge. *He confronts them with God* in a kind of personal immediacy which is without any parallel in the rabbinical literature.[158]

Jesus acts in this way simply because he is on intimate terms with God.[159] Much has been made of his use of the familiar term "Abba" in speaking of God, but I believe that this is not only strained (and, when one reflects on it, silly: did he really mean to call God "Daddy"?) but inaccurate. Far stronger evidence of his unique relationship with God is provided by the fact that despite the peace which he radiated and the evident power of his words, he remained a stranger in the world. There was something profoundly different, something totally "other" about him. In respect to people of his own day it would have to be said that his thoughts were not their thoughts, his ways not their ways. Mark preserves the clearest traces of this (3:21–30; 6:1–6) in stories which were apparently shocking to the later evangelists and which they either edited or omitted. Jesus' own family apparently thought he was crazy, while the religious leaders of his people thought him possessed by a devil and the people of his own town rejected him.

Jesus knows that the stance which men and women take toward him is the stance they take toward God (this is the point of Mark 10:32), and for this reason there is one thing which he seems to want almost desperately: he wants people to *rely* on him, to place their confidence in him. This lends a note of urgency to his call, an element of "drop everything—God is here and it is up to you to do something about it." He confronts everyone he meets with this call, and he expresses its urgency in language so remarkably unreligious that some of it has scandalized generations of Christian preachers. (His words of praise for the crooked foreman in Luke 16:8 are a great example of this.)[160]

4.45　But this immediacy which characterizes Jesus' relationship with God is very strange. He gains nothing from it. He has come to serve and he does not insist on his prerogatives. At every moment he is perfectly confident of who he is—he never undergoes anything like an "identity crisis"—but he is utterly without arrogance. He knows that he is related to God in an absolutely unique way, but he is the most unpompous of men. In fact, he is rather careless about his "honor" and his reputation. He associates with those who are "unclean" according to the ritual law and who are disreputable when judged according to the religious norms of his day (or of ours, for that matter). He seems to be quite unconcerned about the contamination which the law was always trying to avoid. (The story of the leper in Mark 1:40–45 illustrates this very well.)[161] The tax collectors and prostitutes who were among his followers were a scandal to the pious of his day, but he didn't seem to care what people thought. He feels no need to prove anything about himself. If the story of his baptism by John is historical,[162] it would be typical of him—who cares if people think of him as a sinner? None of this is important now (if it ever was) because now God, the real God, is breaking into the world in him.

The mystery remains. It is quite clear that he is not "God" *in the only sense which that word could have had for him and for the New Testament writers who record his word.* Otherwise the amazing text of Mark 10:18 would never have been preserved: "Why do you call me good? Only God is good." Jesus speaks to God as no man ever has, and he acts in God's name with calm confidence as he proclaims the unheard of message of the God who will not allow his mercy to be limited; but God remains the "other" whom he knows and loves, whose will he does, to whom he speaks.[163] However, in him the *real* God acts—a God who had never really shown his face before—and for this reason an old world comes to an end and a new one begins. Even the most intimate human relationships will not remain untouched (Mk 3:31–35). And this new world is full of paradox. Sinners are still sinners and there is no attempt to excuse them or their actions in the name of poor heredity or bad environment, but Jesus invites them into his company precisely *as* sinners, and he implies that by bringing them into his company he is bringing them into the company of God. He calls into question the classic and sacred ways of drawing near to God which were the proudest possession of his people, because the new world which he brings cannot exist with the old world and its ways.[164]

Because of his immediacy to God, when Jesus meets people he brings them into the light and into the truth in an absolutely unique way. The peace which he radiates is the peace which only God can give, and because it is God's peace it cannot be limited to the mind and spirit but reaches out to touch the body, with its various ills and weaknesses. This is the basis of the healings which undoubtedly accompanied Jesus' preaching and which themselves stand as the authentic basis of a miracle tradition which, in its later stages, grew rampant and uncontrolled. Even more striking examples of the way in which Jesus brought people into the truth are provided by stories which show his sharp insight into a situation and into the motives of those involved. He has a sense of just what to say, and when his opponents try to trap him, suddenly they find themselves in the net. The story of the origin of his authority (Mk 11:27–33) is a good example of this, as is his answer to the very dangerous question of paying tribute to Rome.

The final mark of Jesus' uniqueness and of his mysterious relation to God is the fact that he meets each person in the place and in the situation where that person is at the moment. Each human being he meets brings something unique to the encounter—sin, hunger, pain, rejection, sorrow, even superstition; each in his or her own way brings to the meeting some unique aspect of the human tragedy. But they meet Jesus and they are brought into a new world, and they live on a new earth under a new heaven. Through this man who is so totally and exhaustively human they have encountered a God whose existence they never suspected. They have contributed their individuality, their uniqueness to the encounter, and he has contributed his, and as a result they go in peace—a peace that the world cannot give and therefore a peace which the world cannot take away. So it was for them and so it is for us, and that is why Jesus is the Christ, yesterday, today, and the same forever.

4.5   The Task of Christology Today

The task of Christology today can be defined by a question: "How can we think and speak clearly and accurately about Jesus Christ and his mystery?" It is well to remember that we do not ask this question because we have a taste for speculation or because we refuse to be satisfied with simple faith in the Jesus of the Gospels. In the famous scene at Caesarea Philippi it is Jesus himself who poses the question: "Who do people say that I am?" and the question is as valid today as it was then. It is *Jesus* who forces us to raise questions about him and his mystery, and about the mystery of his origin and destiny. It was Jesus himself who was incessantly raising the question of the identity of the real God and continually raising the question of the identity of the real human being who stands before that God. It was Jesus who, in word and work, forced his audience to confront the question of his relationship to God and his relationship to us. Faith is not the blind acceptance of the irrational; it is the persevering attempt to answer these questions which Jesus himself posed, sometimes explicitly, more often implicitly.[165]

But if it is Jesus himself who forces us to ask questions about him and his relationship to God and to us, it remains true that the *form* those questions take has much to do with the way other human beings in the past have tried to answer these questions, and in particular with ways of answering them which won official approval of the Church and which can be called *christological doctrine.* It is this which forces us to ask questions about him such as these: Is God a person (or more than one)? Does Jesus have at his disposal God's own way of knowing? Did Jesus exist as a person before he appeared on earth? Is Jesus a divine person or a human person? If it were not for the christological doctrine which was formulated at Nicaea and then developed by the great Scholastic theologians, these questions, if asked at all today, would, *today,* receive simple and obvious answers.[166] But we, today, have received the faith from those who took the christological dogma and its elaboration in Scholastic theology seriously, and therefore our faith *is not entirely independent of these formulas.* We cannot step over eighteen centuries which have mediated to us the Jesus of the New Testament, nor would it be a healthy sign if we wanted to do so. What I propose to do in the following pages is, first, to present *in outline* a way of thinking and speaking about Jesus and his relationship to God which makes use of the present-day concept of person, and, second, to examine the most important traditional ways of talking about the same problem. I believe that this will make an intelligent assimilation of the New Testament data possible, and I believe that it may also show that the conciliar doctrine itself makes demands upon us which are quite different from those which it is commonly assumed to make.

4.6 God and Jesus: Restating the New Testament Teaching

4.61 In one sense, Jesus brought the good news of the real God whom no one had ever known. His own distinctly unreligious definition of the word "God" gives clear evidence of this. But it is equally true to say that Jesus brought the good news about who the God of the fathers and the God of the prophets *really* was. He revealed the mystery of the God of his people—a mystery not known or clearly foreseen in the Old Testament, but one which nevertheless fulfilled the deepest hope and longing of Old Testament men and women.

In fact, the uniqueness of God in the New Testament lies precisely in this known/unknown character: the God of Abraham, Isaac and Jacob is the God who is the Father of Jesus Christ. Even those New Testament texts which show Jesus and Paul emphasizing the absolute newness of God leave no doubt that this radically new and unpredictable God is the very one who spoke with Moses and whose word came to the prophets. The Old Testament itself had prepared for such a God in the theophany of Exodus 3:14, where God reveals that he is the undefinable one, "who will be who he will be" in his own good time and on his own terms.

The God of the New Testament takes up within himself all of the paradoxes of the Old Testament. He is the one upon whose face no man can look and live, but he loves Israel with a love as passionate and tender as that of a husband for his wife. He is the high and holy one whose thoughts are not our thoughts but at the same time he has loved us with an everlasting love.

However there is an underlying paradox which the Old Testament seems to sense but never articulates. This God, who is no mere "Supreme Being" (how inadequate a title!), but the infinite, pure intensity of being itself,[167] is, on the one hand, without beginning or end, absolutely self-sufficient, in need of no one and no thing. Yet on the other hand he has willed from all eternity not to be alone but to turn to another—a person who will be his counterpart. He is the eternal decision to speak to this other and to hearken to the word which this other speaks. He is the eternal decision to love this other and to accept this other's love.

God(nt) who is eternally self-sufficient wills *not* to be; God who is eternally of and for himself wills to be for another. In a moment of infinite paradox, *God(nt)* remains himself, without loss or diminution, while turning with the infinite intensity of his being toward another, and establishing for eternity the truth which no metaphysics could create or deduce—that to *be* is to be for another.

This infinite paradox in God is one of which we can speak and think only by talking of real distinctions within the divine life, which make possible a number of assertions which would be contradictory in inner-worldly terms. The very one who exists of himself, without reference to anyone or anything outside him, is nevertheless the subject of *two kinds of relatedness* to all that is outside the divine life: he is one whose intelligibility can be embodied, can take form outside him, and he is one who can be present in affirmation, acceptance and love to that which he is not. These two kinds of relatedness are called, in the New Testament itself, *Word* (Logos) and *Spirit* (Pneuma). The second of these terms had a rather long history in Jewish thought— probably centuries older than the account in the Priestly source of Genesis where it appears for the first time.[168] The Jewish and Israelite "pre-history" of the word *Logos* is more complex, but the tradition that Yahweh creates through the power of his word is an ancient and constant motif of Old Testament thought.[169] Specifically Greek philosophical interests are absent from the earlier strata of the Old Testament, but from the beginning the written revelation had to grapple with the problem of a God who is absolutely transcendent yet at the same time really immanent in the world. Characteristically, unlike Greek thought which attempted to deal with the problem by constructing a series of mediators, intermediate beings between God and world, the Hebrew mind accepted the need to speak *dialectically* about God, and used a language which, if used to speak of the things of this world, would be contradictory.

Note carefully that there is nothing in the Old Testament or New Testament which would imply that either Word or Spirit is a *personal counterpart* of *God(nt)* in the modern sense of the word *personal.* To put it accurately, *Word* is the real condition of possibility, within God, for the existence of anyone or anything outside him, and *Spirit* is the condition of possibility for his accepting and loving presence with things and persons outside him. Word and Spirit are the conditions of possibility, within the very life of *God(nt),* for his having a counterpart to whom he could speak and with whom he could be involved in a relation of mutual love. The personalization (in the *modern sense*) of Word and Spirit is not undertaken either by the Old Testament or the New Testament and cannot be justified on the basis of either of these texts. Word and Spirit *are personal* not because they are personal counterparts of the Father within the divine life itself but because they are forms of relatedness which *God(nt)*, a person, has with a person or persons in our world.

But what, then, is the relationship of *God(nt)* to that concept of God which was developed in the conciliar period, particularly from Nicaea to Chalcedon? Are they the same? To identify them can only lead to greater confusion, because there was a *tendency*, already visible before Chalcedon, but destined to become dominant in later centuries, to interpret *God(iv+)* as three-personal (in something like the modern sense—three distinct subjects, each with his own consciousness and will, and each capable of engaging in dialogue with the others). If *God(iv+)* had simply been seen as one who had three distinct forms of relatedness to creation (and especially to personal beings), then *God(iv+)* and *God(nt)* could have been identified, but certain associations of the Latin translation of "hypostasis" (*persona*)[170] gave *God(iv+)* a meaning which is not easy to reconcile with the New Testament. *God(nt)* is, in the *modern* sense, one person, not three.

Furthermore, there was a growing tendency in theology, after Chalcedon, to use the word "God" to refer to the divine "nature"—that is, to the complex of qualities and attributes which are at the disposal of the divine "persons" (thought of as three distinct subjects). But such a "nature" is not the God of the New Testament to whom Jesus spoke and prayed and who said to Jesus, "You are my Son."

4.62 Note carefully that in the New Testament it is not the Logos or *Word* which is the personal counterpart of God and the term of his eternal decision not to remain alone. *Jesus* is the counterpart of *God(nt)*, the one whom he has sought and found.

The world and its history, natural and human, came into being,
so that God might one day greet Jesus as his Son.

God's will to find a counterpart, another to whom he might
speak and for whose answering word he might listen, is a call
which is spoken from the infinite fullness of his own being into
the infinite emptiness of that which is outside him. Creation is
the meeting place of two infinities—the boundless fullness of
God's being and the measureless emptiness of that which is not
God.[171] Creation, so understood, is not a single, discrete event
that results in an inert "thing" which then continues to exist
under its own power. Created being lacks the power to maintain
or explain itself; there is nothing ordinary about it and it is
anything but self-explanatory. Its equilibrium is threatened and
it exists in a state of almost inconceivable tension between its
tendency to revert to nothingness and its striving toward the
one who has summoned it to be. Creation is a "coming to be"—
a movement from the emptiness, the "otherness" and disper-
sion of non-being toward the fullness of being to which it is
called. Created being is forever marked by its twofold origin; it
is always on the way from non-being toward God. Its existence is
real but threatened; it exists, but only in total dependence.

4.63 In this light, creation ought to be seen as a progressive
event, in the sense that created being develops and becomes
more complex by adapting to the demands of new environ-
ments. A brief reflection on this fact might indicate how the
Christology outlined here can deal with the universality of Jesus
Christ and with the question of his relationship to the countless
millions who have never heard and will never hear his name.

The process of becoming more complex is really a process
of becoming more fully real and of existing more intensely.[172]
This process covers an immense span of time. The initial response to the creative word of God is quite feeble and tentative;

the first existing things are merely material: fragmented, disparate, incommunicado. They exist, but they lack consciousness
and spontaneity. However, the creative call of God is insistent;
what he has called into being does not slip back into nothingness, but grows in wholeness, unity and integration. With the
passage of time, simpler forms of life appear out of earlier, non-
living forms (and their appearance is no greater and no less a
"miracle" than the coming to be of the first atom with its
accompanying framework of space and time). Under the inces-
sant summons of the divine word, the first tentative steps toward
knowledge and freedom are made: animal life appears, with the
consciousness and spontaneity proper to itself. Now the world
moves more quickly and surely toward unification. But development does not stop, and in time beings appear who are open,
consciously, to all that is—beings who can know the truth and
love it and do it. The call of God continues, and one day, out of
the race of those whose glory is their hope of infinity, there
comes a person who can turn in full recognition to the one from
whom the call has come. In this person, the call of God which
has gone forth from all eternity, the call of God for another who
is *like* him and *of* him (the call for a *Son*) is answered. In him, all
of the partial answers to God's call which were found in the
earlier stages of pre-historic and historic development find their
fulfillment, and in the complexity of the life of this one who is
Son, all the earlier stages of cosmos and world are taken up and
find their meaning.

4.64 This one, in whom the call which was spoken in eternity
receives a final and definitive answer, is Jesus of Nazareth. This
man is the answer to God's eternal decision not to be alone. In
him God finds one "in his image and likeness" and to whom he
can therefore speak the words: "You are my Son." But the one
to whom God speaks these words is a human person, a man of
authentic human spontaneity and freedom, and so there are

other words which must be spoken: "Will you be my Son?" The word of God to Jesus is at once assertion and request, and it is in his willingness to accept God as Father and to define himself only as his Son that the creative call of God receives a fitting response. It is the *freedom of Jesus* which is the perfect counterpart of the *omnipotence of God.*

Jesus is the one who accepts God as Father, as the one *of whom* and *from whom* he is. This free decision of Jesus is the act of *letting God be God.* In eternity God has willed not to be alone but to speak to another and wait for his response. This eternal will to be Father becomes irrevocable and definitive in history when Jesus becomes *this Son,* and the world will never be the same. At this moment history finds its center, and the sole purpose of existence is that all may be conformed to the likeness of this Son, that all may be sons and daughters of this God. God who *is* in eternity has *become,* in time, something which he was not. In Jesus, God is really committed to history; in him, God has entrusted himself to the historical process; in him, God has entered history.

If this free response had been refused, then all creation from the beginning up to this moment would have lost its *raison d'être.* What would have become of it? Would it have sunk back into nothingness, so that God might have issued his call again in another world, another universe? To attempt to answer this question is probably useless speculation. The world of the possibles is not real; the only real world is the one determined by the freedom of Jesus and by our freedom. Jesus *gave* the answer and called God Father as no one had before and no one could again. He is the response in history to the eternal call, and he is a response to God which is *like* God and *of* God. If *Word* is that element or aspect of God which makes it possible for him to find an image and likeness outside himself, then Jesus is the term or result in history of this Word; *he is the Word of God in history.* The relation of Jesus Christ to God is the *fact,* of which the coexistence of different *kinds of relatedness* in God is the eternal possibility.

Speculation on the mystery of God and Jesus is not justified either by its daring or by its depth. As always it must be measured by the word of God in the New Testament, where that word reached a form in which it can play a critical role in faith and life. The very brief outline of a speculative Christology which has been presented in these few pages has been formulated in terms which cannot be found in the text of the New Testament, but it will not be inappropriate to indicate certain interests and concerns of at least some of the New Testament writings, which are taken seriously by the outline suggested here.

First, the New Testament knows of a "pre-history" of Jesus, and the fact that the Christian Church adopted the Old Testament as its own sacred book (even before the New Testament was completed) is striking evidence of this. In accordance with the customs and views of the age, certain New Testament writers (Matthew in particular) present Jesus as the fulfillment of Old Testament prophecies. They do this in a way which we cannot repeat today, because it is evident that they are not really interpreting Old Testament texts, but finding a meaning in them which the texts themselves did not have and of which their writers were not aware. But once these "predictions" are set aside as such, it becomes possible to ask whether they are not simply an historically conditioned way of asserting a profound truth: *the fact that Jesus is the fulfillment of all that is authentic in the hopes and dreams of men and women of the Old Testament.* The Old Testament is the pre-history of Jesus, the last preparatory step before that central moment of history which was constituted by the appearance of the man who is nothing less than the Son of God.

The New Testament, precisely in its explicit[173] and implicit acceptance of the Old Testament, asserts that the world before

Jesus pointed toward him, prepared the way for him and waited for him. In doing this, the New Testament also accepts the pre-history of Israel, as found sporadically in different Old Testament texts, and as found formally and explicitly in the patriarchal narratives and the primeval history of the J tradition in Genesis.[174] The immanent dynamisms of the world which antedated Judaism and of human pre-history itself come to fulfillment in Jesus.

But there are more specific references than this. In the (in my view) post-Pauline Epistles to the Colossians and the Ephesians we can find some remarkable texts which point to the historic and cosmic significance of Jesus Christ. Colossians 1:15 refers to him, for example, as "the image of the unseen God, the first-born of all creation; everything came into being through him . . . and for him; he was before all and everything has its meaning in him."[175] Some of the words used in the Greek text are difficult to translate exactly, but the text as a whole is a relatively clear assertion of the fact that all that exists achieves its goal and purpose in Jesus Christ, who is, at the same time, the first-born in a new world. The Epistle to the Colossians here resumes a characteristically Pauline theme—that of Jesus Christ as the second Adam and the initiator of a new humanity.

However, it is in Paul's Epistle to the Romans that we find most clearly stated the conviction that God's commitment to the world and to us becomes definitive and historically real in Jesus Christ. For Paul, God is the one who *lays claim to us* [176] while we are sinners and still estranged from him. God's justifying act is not merely something that he *does;* rather, God is *essentially* the one who lays claim to the sinner, and this is what it means to be God. Paul's word *dikaiosune* (usually rendered as "justice"—a rather unfortunate translation) really means the *exercise of God's power* in a definitive way. Since no English word can capture the meaning, only a paraphrase will do: *dikaiosune* is God himself, insofar as he asserts his rights over a fallen world. It is an act in which he asserts that, regardless of what is proper, regardless of what we deserve, we belong to him.[177] For Paul, it is Christ who reveals this power of God, particularly in his death. But note that the revelation spoken of here is not information newly released about what was really the case all along. In Romans 3:21ff Paul uses an expression (*nuni de*) which implies that the definitive moment in history has come: the world will never be the same again and *neither will God.* To translate verse 21 by saying that the justice of God *has appeared* is to miss the point. The Greek form *pephanerotai* means "has put in an appearance and *is really here.*" The point is not that God was always this way and that now we have finally been allowed to see it; rather the point is that something new has happened and that God is laying claim to all creation in a radically different way. A good way of paraphrasing Paul's thought would be to say that *in Jesus God is now here as one who has definitively asserted his rights over us.* In Jesus, and precisely because Jesus is his Son, God becomes in fact what he previously was in intention and in his eternal will: a God of love and not of wrath.[178]

To present in detail this important side of Paul's thought would be the work of at least another book. In summary, at least this should be said: Paul is a Jew and knows that the reality of God is his commitment to history. We know God not by reflecting on his immutable essence but by hearkening to his voice, by seeing his historical action and by becoming part of his creative engagement with the world and with human beings. For Paul, no one less than God himself is at stake in Jesus. In Jesus, God becomes truly, finally, definitively God, because in him God has reconciled the world to himself.

4.65 The view of the relationship of Jesus and God which I have begun to outline here has a superficial resemblance to a teaching called *adoptionism*. The latter is a serious distortion of

Christian faith which has been solemnly rejected by the Church on a number of occasions.[179] It lies at the opposite end of the spectrum from the other basic christological heresy—docetism—but both spring from the same source: *the refusal to let God take history so seriously that our history becomes quite literally God's history.* Docetism isolates God from historical involvement by rejecting the reality of Jesus Christ's humanity; for the docetist, Jesus merely seems to be human, but in reality is not. Adoptionism isolates God from history by insisting that Jesus is a mere man who is not really the personal counterpart of God but who, because of his moral qualities, is treated by God *as if* he were his Son. Both heresies preserve the infinite distance between God and man by rejecting any real historical involvement on the part of God.[180] For both, God is really a benevolent spectator who looks in a kindly way at the human situation, but in no sense is he an actor, really engaged on the scene of history.

Against adoptionism this must be made clear: in no sense of the word can Jesus ever be called a "mere man" (although it is questionable that any human being ever should!). But Jesus is, in a most fundamental way which bears directly on his human personality, unique. In Jesus, God seeks and finds his own counterpart, the image and likeness of *himself*. He is the very presence of God's "glory"—a term which came to Paul from the Old Testament, where it means *the manifest presence of God.* This human being, this human person, Jesus, does not achieve some sort of moral perfection which is then rewarded by God with an "as if" sonship. Jesus achieves the fullness of personal growth, the full power of human personality, in confrontation and dialogue with the infinite mystery, the infinite person, who has no beginning and no end. Jesus becomes a person in the full and final sense in the encounter with God. Jesus is not merely a human person of whom God approves. He is one who becomes irrevocably himself in knowing and loving God (always here in the New Testament sense)—in being able to say "Father" to him. In all of his words and acts which recognize God as Father, he becomes and remains God's counterpart, the person whom God sought from all eternity. In and through the events at the end of Jesus' life, the personal relationship between Father and Son becomes complete, unsurpassable, final.[181]

But note well: Jesus' personal relationship with God cannot be relegated to a place "outside" the world and to a time which preceded the concrete human existence of Jesus. Jesus is the only Son of this Father, precisely in his human existence. Jesus' relationship to the Father is not grounded in some timeless substratum of his being which would underlie his outer human reality. What is eternal, "pre-existent" (the term is unfortunate), is the Word of God, which is *not,* in the *contemporary sense of the word,* the person of Jesus, but is rather God's eternal commitment to be personally present in history. Because God's word is a distinct form of relatedness within the very life of God, history can be *God's own history.* And one good way to describe Jesus would be to call him the reality of the history of God. Jesus is the proof that God cannot be kept out of history and that history has no meaning apart from the presence of God as a participant within it.[182]

4.66 Jesus is God's commitment to the world and to us, and it follows that God himself is knowable and real for us only in the historical concreteness of Jesus. But it is not merely a question of God's reality for us, as though it were possible to make a neat distinction between God's being in itself and God's being for us. God *himself* is the eternal decision not to be alone but to communicate *his own being* in history. God himself is really real, in a definitive, "worldly" way (that is, in the way he wants to be) only in Jesus.[183] On the basis of the New Testament's own understanding of the word *God,* we can be quite reserved in calling Jesus *God,* but on that same basis we can confidently say that *God* *for us is Jesus*—and is there any other God but the God who is for us?

The mystery of Jesus is that in him God communicates himself in a full and unrestricted way. The divinity of Jesus is not some kind of second substance in him, some type of superior reality which would have to be thought of as "next to" and necessarily in competition with his human reality. Jesus' divinity consists in the fact that he is the human person (in the *contemporary sense* of *person*) who is the perfect counterpart of God and who is therefore *the manifestation and presence of God himself in the world.* [184]

As the human person who is the counterpart of God, Jesus knows that in accepting God as Father, he is the Son whom God has sought from all eternity. As Son, Jesus is the realization in history of the Logos or Word, which is God's eternal commitment to the world of space and time. But Jesus is one person; there are not two "acting centers" in him, one human and one divine, who would inevitably engage in dialogue with each other. [185] Jesus cannot and must not be split. He does not engage in dialogue with the Logos or Word but with *God* (in the New Testament sense), with the Father. [186] Jesus is *what* he is and Jesus is *who* he is, not because his human nature confronts the divine nature or the person of the Logos, but because Jesus Christ is constituted in his entirety as a person through his personal relationship with God, that is, with his Father.

Jesus is not to be thought of as the "place" where the Logos, descending from on high, encounters the concrete humanity of Jesus. Such a view would place the mystery of Jesus in the fact that within him, separate and conflicting entities would somehow be joined together. Attempts to do this are always patchwork; they have the appearance of piety about them and they do not lack a certain brilliance and subtlety, but they distort the real mystery of Jesus: the fact that this man, in his concrete historical reality, is the "you" to whom God speaks with the fullness of personal commitment, is the person whom God willed to encounter, and in whom God finds one to know and to love.

Jesus himself does not have to confront the problem of two distinct consciousnesses which would coexist in him and which would have to be harmonized or reconciled with each other. Jesus is never confronted with the ridiculous question of how much knowledge he can legitimately allow into his human consciousness from out of his divine consciousness. Jesus has one consciousness, a human one, as befits a human person, and with this human consciousness he is aware of who God really is for him. He is aware of the fatherly word of God which is spoken to him and which asks him, precisely as a human being, to be really *Son,* and therefore to be the one whom the Father has sought as his counterpart from all eternity. The vision of God which Jesus possessed[187] has to be interpreted this way: in him the "I-you" relationship which the Father wills comes into being, becomes history. He knows God as his Father. Other interpretations of the beatific vision which Jesus was assumed to possess either require a miraculous suspension of the natural effects of the heavenly vision of God (so that Jesus can both see God and suffer intensely) or they trivialize the suffering of Jesus and make it into a great bit of acting which he engaged in "in order to give us good example" (whatever that might mean under the circumstances!).

4.67 The mystery of Jesus is the mysterious fact that God's commitment to history is real. History is not the manifestation of what has been decided in eternity. The future is not real before it occurs. Neither the future (what *will* come to pass), the possible (what *might* come to pass) nor the futurible (what human beings *would* freely choose *if* they were put in certain circumstances) has any kind of ideal existence in the thought of God.[188] God knows the *real,* and the future *is* real only when it is enacted within history by his creatures, operating within the limits of the spontaneity and power available to them. Our real future is constituted by our free choices, and God's commitment to it and knowledge of it is *identical* with his commitment to us and to our real freedom. We are historical beings because the future decides who we are, and because in really essential matters, our future is in our hands. God's commitment to history is his commitment to *his own future,* and this commitment of his is the concrete reality we call Jesus Christ. In the life, death and ongoing life of Jesus Christ, God became and is becoming in space and time the one he wills to be from all eternity.

God's choice, God's stance, God's election of man and the world is decided in history, and it is in Jesus that God makes this decision.[189] God himself has become historical in Jesus, and it is the resurrection which makes this evident once and for all. Jesus as a full and integral human person is the consequence of God's will to reveal himself. This is true not in the sense that God first decides to reveal himself and then looks around at various possibilities and finally chooses one of them; God does not look *into* the world and into human history to find an appropriate vehicle in which to reveal himself. Rather, the world itself and the history of man within the world are the form taken by God's eternal decision not to be alone. There is an infinite qualitative difference between God and the world, and yet when God enters history in Jesus Christ, this does not represent the arrival of an alien being. In Jesus the world finds its own fulfillment— the one for which it was made and toward which all of its immanent dynamisms strive.[190]

In Jesus God fashions his definitive relationship with the world and the world's definitive relationship with him. In Jesus we are given the power to live in the presence of God who is, once and for all, certainly and irrevocably, our Father. In the presence of such a God we can live in joy and die in peace; our only task is to *let him be for us* the God he wants to be—and this is an excellent definition of faith.[191] We let him be the one he wants to be by hearkening to his word, and when we do, we find that it is a word which heals and saves. As hearers of this word we can live in the freedom which is proper to those who are sons and daughters of this God and whose historical destiny finally has meaning. The real God does not transport us to some secure haven above the world and outside time. We remain those who are in history and therefore have a past, a present and a future, but for hearers of the word of God the meaning of these three dimensions of time changes radically: the guilt which we feel about the past loses all power to destroy us, the doubt we feel about the significance of our present choices yields to hope, and the anxiety we feel about the future yields to the certainty of eternal life.

In the fullest sense, God's commitment to history is the real freedom of Jesus. This does not mean that God is committed to indifference or to arbitrary choices (which are "free" only in the sense they are not determined by any motives, rational or irrational). It does not mean that God's commitment to freedom, either that of Jesus or our own, is the giving of a *carte blanche*. Freedom does not consist in the power to do different things, to act or not to act, to act in this or that way. *Freedom is the act of willing, wanting, choosing the truth which transcends every concrete and individual situation (but which is found within all such situations). Freedom is the decision to be open to reality, to think and act intelligently.*[192] Freedom, properly understood, is not the indifference in virtue of which we can do good or evil. To act freely is to act well, and it is the refusal of freedom which is evil. The mystery of evil is not the mystery of freedom but the mystery of our power to *refuse* freedom. If Jesus' freedom were his power to do right or wrong, it would be hard to understand how the exercise of that freedom would engage God in the world. But Jesus' freedom is not this; it is his act of letting God be for him the one he wanted to be from eternity, and in this event the world comes to fulfillment and God becomes definitively real in inner-worldly terms—the very terms on which he eternally wished his reality to rest.

4.7   The Traditional Problems and Solutions of Christology

In the past, the questions about Jesus Christ and the answers to those questions have been very different from those I outlined above. In general, the questions have originated in Chalcedon's teaching about the two natures of Christ, and the answers have been developed by trying to show how these two natures, while remaining distinct, are nevertheless united in the concrete individual Jesus Christ. In a world without any real understanding of or sympathy for the category of history, in a world for which the very notion of a truly historical God would be anathema, the classic teaching on the two natures of Christ was the only possible way of safeguarding Christian faith from docetism on the one hand (which denies that Jesus is a real human being) and from adoptionism on the other (which denies that in encountering Jesus we encounter no other than God himself). For these reasons, Chalcedon's teaching on the two natures was necessary. Over and above this, the truth which Chalcedon intended to safeguard must be affirmed and protected by any Christology, present or future. But without calling these facts into question, we have to be equally clear about another fact: Chalcedon's teaching on the two natures of Christ was a means to an indispensable end, but it was not an end in itself.[193] This does not imply that the teaching of the council was false or may someday become false, but it does leave open one possibility: that better ways of safeguarding the one thing necessary (the fact that the man Jesus Christ is the real presence of God among us) may now be available as the result of the emergence of new forms of thought and language during the past fifteen hundred years. In the preceding pages I have indicated how it is possible to speak of Jesus and his relationship with God, using a conceptual framework quite different from that employed by the bishops at Chalcedon. I make no apology for this, because it is the same process we must engage in if we are to understand the text of Scripture itself today. These theses about God and Jesus are an attempt to do what systematic theology should do, that is, make it possible for us to be addressed again by the New Testament. They do this because they show us that some of the things which faith seemed to demand were really not part of faith but could be traced not only to rather questionable interpretations of the New Testament but to equally questionable interpretations of the conciliar documents and of official Church teaching. However, the practice of reading the New Testament through conciliar glasses (that is, regarding it as a source book for answers to questions which emerged hundreds of years after the New Testament was written) has resulted in a large body of interpretations of conciliar teaching, and in ways of looking at Jesus Christ which are still influential in preaching, catechetics and Christian piety today. Behind terminology such as *consubstantial with the Father, hypostatic union, kenosis,* and *pre-existence,* and behind traditional discussion of problems such as that of the consciousness or the freedom of Jesus, there often lies a tacit understanding of Jesus Christ which can make it almost impossible to ask the right questions. The fact that the tacit understanding mentioned here is not articulated makes no difference; in fact, the failure to articulate it is quite harmful, because it remains unconscious and therefore cannot be subjected to criticism—either that of systematic theology or that of the word of God itself. The classical terms, problems and discussions of Christology need to be examined, and in doing this we should keep two questions in mind—first, "What is the substance, the heart of the matter, which these formulas are attempting to safeguard?" and second, "What is there in these terms and problems and discussions which reflects the linguistic and philosophical resources of certain periods of history but which is scarcely intelligible today?" One of the major tasks of systematic theology is to provide a good critique of language.[194] Good exegesis provides such a critique for Scripture, and it makes no sense to cultivate a (pseudo-) reverence for the conciliar and theological tradition which is evidently not demanded by the New Testament word itself.

4.71 In the preceding pages I have attempted to state what I see as the substance of Christology: that this man Jesus is the very word and presence of the Father among us, that he is in an absolutely unique sense *of* God and *from* God and that he is therefore in just as unique a sense the *Son* of God. However, Greek ways of looking at God and man gave rise to problems and solutions which have made it difficult to find this Jesus in the New Testament. Briefly, the development went something like this.

It was clear from the entire New Testament that the same Jesus Christ who had lived on earth and who had died was now "with God" in the sense of sharing God's own life. He now has a new mode of being and of acting. At times, Paul and John talk as though this divine mode of being was something that Jesus had before he became man and lived his earthly life.[195] We will examine the meaning and the interpretation of this later and will concentrate on that fact which seems to belong to the earliest preaching: that there were two successive stages in Jesus' life— one in which he lived in the human sphere and another in which he lived, after his death, in the divine sphere.

For the Greek mind, as we have often noted in this book, man changes but God is immutable. Therefore, if Jesus Christ belongs to *both* spheres, the human and the divine, then two different "things" or principles must be found within him to account for the fact that contradictory statements have to be made about him (for example, "he changes" and "he is unchangeable"). When Nicaea stated that he was consubstantial with the Father, of the same substance as the Father, and that he *was* God, this could mean only one thing to the Greek mind: that in him the "substance," the *underlying reality* of God was present. It was evidently assumed at Nicaea that Jesus was human and that he therefore shared the same underlying reality as we do, although some time passed before this would be stated in the form "consubstantial with us."[196] In addition, as a consequence of Nicaea's statement that *he* was God and had the same "nature" as the Father, there will be a *tendency* to find the divine element in him precisely in that which makes him an acting subject. This tendency was certainly present at Chalcedon, but here it should be noted that the meaning "conscious, acting subject" belonged by right not to the Greek *hypostasis,* but to the Latin *persona* (although even here the notion of "distinct individual consciousness"—the modern sense of *person*—had not been attained by *persona*). However, it may well be that Leo the Great and the Latin tradition after him had an understanding of the Trinity as distinct persons (in the modern sense), capable of engaging in dialogue with each other, which went somewhat beyond the doctrine formally stated at Chalcedon.

Now if Jesus Christ is divine, precisely as a conscious and free subject, then as such it would be necessary, in the Greek view, that this divine subject *pre-exist* his human life. He cannot come to be a person, because such a development is excluded from God by Greek standards. Of course, the notion of pre-existence was by no means merely an invention of the conciliar period. Both Paul and John had tried to deal with the mystery of the unity of Jesus and God by making use of the concept of pre-existence,[197] although the pre-existence of *Jesus Christ* is not precisely what was being affirmed in the prologue to John's Gospel, and the Pauline text which seems most clearly to imply pre-existence was probably adapted by Paul from a tradition which antedated him, and whose mythological elements he neither bothered nor cared to excise. Remember, too, that the notion of pre-existence was part of the world-view of very many of the bishops who met at Nicaea, and *precisely for this reason should not be regarded as something which they formally affirmed;* many of them, as good Origenists, were convinced that the souls of *all* human beings pre-existed their birth!

When Jesus is thought of as a divine, pre-existent person, this has an immediate effect on the way in which Jesus' humanity is viewed: Jesus' mystery is thought of as that of *incarnation*—the process in which a divine person acquires "flesh," a human way of acting, a human nature.[198] This mystery in turn will be explained by the concept of *hypostatic union,* in which the divine person is the bond which brings together and holds together the disparate natures. Since, in this so-called "hypostatic" union, the divine person assumes the attributes of a human being, the question arises about how a divine being can lay aside his divine prerogatives, "empty" himself of them, in order to become human. This problem of *kenosis* as presented here is quite typically Greek, although the verb form itself had been used by Paul in the famous text of Philippians 2:5–11. Note here the typically Greek presupposition: human and divine attributes are essentially contradictory, and the human attributes as such are *negative* and constitute a kind of threat or affront to divine being.

Finally, as a result of asking and answering questions of this kind, still other questions will be raised about the consciousness and freedom of Jesus, and it will be affirmed that because he has two complete *natures,* he has *two consciousnesses, two intellects and two wills.* This in turn will raise questions about the relationship between the two members of each pair: How is this one person to be thought of, who disposes of two distinct consciousnesses? How does he keep knowledge out of one consciousness while thinking about it in the other? What does it mean for *one person* to know something in his divine consciousness and to be ignorant of it in his human consciousness?[199]

Most of these questions arose, not because they were implicit in the New Testament material but because they were suggested or demanded by Greek ways of thinking of God and man. But remember that the order in which these problems and pseudo-problems arose should not be limited to the simplified outline presented here. In the genesis and "solution" of pseudo-problems, as in the genesis and solution of real problems, there is a phenomenon called "positive feedback." Thus, an incarnational Christology is not only the *result* of thinking of Jesus Christ as the pre-existent one, but it also fosters speculation on the pre-existence of Christ. In the same way, theorizing about the hypostatic union is at once the result of the doctrine of the two natures and at the same time it implies and imposes a certain interpretation of the doctrine of the two natures which may be considerably narrower than the one intended by those who formulated the original doctrine.[200]

4.8   The Success and Failure of Chalcedon

All of these considerations lead to a somewhat paradoxical conclusion: the only formula which could have succeeded at Chalcedon and which was needed to bring to an end a century and a half of dissension and debate has been at the root of a number of insoluble problems since then. A brief analysis of the problems connected with the "two natures" formula will make it possible to deal with the questions mentioned above: the consubstantiality of Jesus Christ with God, the hypostatic union, kenosis, and, finally, the consciousness and freedom of Jesus Christ. This enumeration and analysis of the problems connected with the doctrine of the two natures is particularly important for one reason: from the medieval period up to the very recent past (that is, during the period of Scholasticism and neo-Scholasticism) it was commonly felt that the task of Christology was to elaborate ever more subtle variations on the teaching of

Chalcedon. In fact, no one suggested that Christology might have any point of departure other than the Chalcedonian definition. Instead, the tacit assumption was that Chalcedon, like the other councils, offered a more objective and accurate treatment of the mystery of Christ than did the New Testament itself.[201]

4.81 The following are some of the areas in which the doctrine of the two natures of Christ has created problems. They are, of course, not insoluble, but they are serious enough to force us to raise a good question: Is the terminology of Chalcedon really essential for the integral statement of Christian faith today?

The word *nature* itself is troublesome. The mere fact that we *speak* of a divine and a human nature in Jesus Christ leads us to believe that the word *nature* has a meaning which is applicable in the same sense to God and to man. It is not enough to note that any trained theologian knows that there are no concepts which are applicable to God and man in the same sense. First of all, most Christians are not trained theologians, and, second, the attempt to speak of God in terms which are applied univocally to things of this world can lull even the trained theologian into the belief that the *same kind* of assertion is being made about God and man—in this case, that *nature* has a meaning which is applicable in the same sense to God and man. But there are no general concepts which have the same meaning when applied to both. Divine nature and human nature are not two specifically different varieties which come under the one generic concept of *nature,* but the use of the same word runs the risk of disguising this fact: the divine nature becomes a well-defined way of acting which, like the human nature, is at the disposal of the second person of the Trinity. But there is nothing in God which is capable of being "well-defined"; at every moment of history he determines in sovereign freedom who he will be at that moment.[202]

Although the Latin word *natura* originally referred to a

principle of action or operation, when the term came to be used
in the doctrine of the "two natures" it acquired a much more
static meaning—in fact *nature* came to be interpreted as a synonym of *substantia,* "substance," that which is constant in the
midst of change. Finally, in much of the theological tradition,
natura and "nature" came to be a collective term for a group of
qualities or attributes. Quite early in the history of christological
speculation a tendency appears to *separate* the divine and human
attributes of Jesus. Once they are separated, those attributes
which are somewhat passive or inert will be attributed to the
"human nature," and those which are active and dynamic will be
attributed to the "divine nature." In such a scheme it is inevitable that the two natures seem to be *juxtaposed,* and the divine
nature seems to be concealed behind the human nature, which
has the power to manifest it or make it present. It is hard to
avoid the impression that in such a view there is a divine being
"somewhere" in Jesus who is pulling the strings, or who is
acting, "giving good example" for our benefit.[203]

4.82 In many ways the doctrine of the two natures seems to
divide Jesus Christ. It is clear from the New Testament that the
encounter of Jesus with *God(nt)* is of absolute importance for all
human beings and constitutes the center of history. But the
doctrine of the two natures suggests that this most significant
encounter should be found not between Jesus and *God(nt),* but
within Jesus Christ, between his divine and human natures. This
was quite congenial to the Greek mind, with its ever-present
interest in the divinization of our common human nature by
contact with the divine nature in Christ. The harm that it could
cause is evident from the neo-Scholastic theology manuals and
the way they treated such themes as the agony in the garden, the
temptations of Jesus, and his obedience to the Father. In these
cases the manuals speak of Jesus (the second Person of the
Trinity!) as being fearful, tempted, submissive, etc. in his human

nature. But this human nature was able to overcome its fear and submit to "God" (that is, *God(iv+—the common divine nature*) and accept its fate. The temptations of Jesus are handled in the same way: as *"God"(iv+)*, of course, he cannot be tempted, but as man he is tempted. Of course, since the human nature coexists in Jesus with his divine nature, in the final analysis Jesus is impregnable. In fact, all examples of Jesus' obedience are really attributed to his humanity, because in the neo-Scholastic view it would be inappropriate for God (post-Nicene again) to obey. And because of the insistence in this tradition that Jesus is God, *the place in which this obedience occurs is within Jesus: Jesus as man obeys Jesus as God!*

It would be difficult to imagine any way of more effectively dividing and dehumanizing Jesus. In this absurd construction (which was often implied to be the mystery of the incarnation!), Jesus ceases to be the *person* who is wholly related to *God(nt)* and instead he becomes the place where the encounter between *God(iv+)* and man takes place. But when Jesus is viewed in this way, the very encounter in which Jesus experiences himself as a person and in which *God(nt)* is present and manifest is replaced by a psychological and ontological monstrosity. It should be noted that there is not one single shred of evidence in the New Testament for any dialogue within Jesus, between his humanity and his divinity or between "Jesus as man" and "Jesus as God." The *New Testament Jesus* faces the *New Testament God.* He speaks to him and he hearkens to his word, and he does this as a fully, exhaustively human being. He becomes, definitively, this human person in his encounter with *God(nt)* and he should not be stripped of his human personality in the interests of a theology which is, if the truth were told, quite embarrassed by the New Testament witness and quite amazed that *God(iv+)* could have waited so long to transform the rathe inaccurate and dangerous formulas of Scripture into the lucid objectivity of Nicaea and Chalcedon.[204]

4.83   Such a parody of Christology was not intended by Chalcedon or by all of the theologians who have repeated that creed and pondered its meaning ever since. But, here again, the old problem with the Greek categories of thought returns: the very concepts which were necessary if docetism and adoptionism were to be avoided moved necessarily, in virtue of their inner dynamic, toward the division of Jesus Christ. But when Jesus is divided, *God (as the New Testament understands the word!) becomes inaccessible.* Jesus is the way, the truth and the life, and no one comes to the Father but through him. But if Jesus is not allowed to be himself, then the one event which leads to the mystery of *God(nt)*—that is, the encounter of Jesus Christ with *God(nt)* who is his Father—is lost sight of and the faceless God of the philosophers has replaced the God who is the Father of Jesus Christ. To a significant degree this may have happened in modern times, and we ought ask insistently if the "God" who is so commonly rejected by people today might not be the real *God(nt)* at all, but might instead be the one who replaces him, as often as men turn aside from the real Jesus in the name of philosophical constructions which are totally alien to the New Testament. If such a "God" is moribund, or even dead, can we, as Christians, mourn his demise?[205]

4.9   Problems with Some Classical Terms

Many of the questions which have traditionally dominated the christological discussion have their origin in the two-natures doctrine of the Council of Chalcedon, and many of these questions have led, because of the philosophical presuppositions they imply, to a narrowing or hardening of the two-natures doctrine itself. It will be useful now to examine some of these questions and terms and indicate how the Christology which I propose in this book can deal with the same problems while avoiding some of the unnecessary and even dangerous implications.

4.91 It would be good to begin with Nicaea's assertion that Jesus Christ, the Son and Word of *God(nt)* is *homoousion to patri.* (Here, I will assume that "consubstantial" or "of the same substance" is an acceptable translation of *homoousion.*) Nicaea's assertion was taken up by Chalcedon, and this latter council interpreted it in the sense that Jesus Christ has the same divine nature as the Father—a nature which coexisted in him with his other nature, the human nature which he shares with us. These statements are necessary and true only if three conditions are fulfilled. The first condition is *that the problem of Jesus' relationship with God(nt) and with us must be approached by raising the question of the nature(s) and/or substance(s) in Jesus*—questions about *what* they are and *how many* they are. The second condition is *that these questions must be accepted as valid and that an answer must be found which employs the same terms as those in which the questions were raised.* The third condition is *that the terms in which questions were raised and answers given are intelligible to those who hear these statements and who are asked to repeat them.* These three conditions were fulfilled for a large number of Christians throughout the Roman empire from the fourth to the sixth centuries of our era. They were not fulfilled in New Testament times and they are not fulfilled today. What was a concrete necessity for Greeks of the fourth to the sixth centuries is no longer either a necessity or a possibility for us.

We are not called upon today to recite formulas which are only marginally intelligible. We are called upon to maintain the *same faith* which Nicaea and Chalcedon strove to maintain, and this may not only *allow* us to use different words to express this faith, but it may actually *demand* it. In an earlier section of this chapter, several theses were proposed which dealt with the relationship between *God(nt)* and Jesus. I believe that these theses now make it possible to address the *same problem* as that addressed by Chalcedon in the term "nature," but to do it in a different terminology and one which is far more effective today.

The truth about Jesus Christ is that he is *with God(nt)* and *God(nt)* is *with* him in a way which is unique and qualitatively different from the way other human beings are present to God. In *this* sense, Jesus is emphatically not a "mere man." To put it simply, Jesus does not stand *outside* the very life of God, but *within* it.[206] We can preserve this all-important truth effectively by asserting that there is nothing in Jesus, *next to,* or *coexisting with* his humanity which accounts for this sharing of the divine life; *nothing apart from his very humanity, his human personality (in our modern sense of the term) is the bearer of his unique relation of sonship.* There is no need to find something immutable in Jesus on which to base the assertion that he lives the very life of God, because the real God is not the immutable "God" of Greek thought. Jesus shares the life of God because he is, precisely as this human being, the counterpart of God. His living of the very life of God is rooted in the Father's decision to speak to him and to hearken to him, to find in him that personal "other" whom God willed from eternity to find. He, *in his humanity,* is the realization of God's eternal commitment of *himself* to history.

The Nicene creed and other professions of faith bind us, not to the philosophical presuppositions of those who wrote them, but rather to the faith which they sought to express. Creeds have not been given to us to free us from the task of understanding, but to challenge us to state in terms which are understandable *today* the same content which was stated in the creed in terms which were understandable *then.* We do not have faith in *statements* but in the reality which they strive to express. The truth about Jesus is that in him, in his concrete human reality and personality, God commits not another, but *himself.* When we encounter Jesus, we meet one who does not observe or admire the divine life from a particularly advantageous stand-point *outside* it; we meet one who, as a human person, is the personal counterpart of the living *God(nt)*. Beyond doubt this is a mystery, but it is not the mystery of a demigod (whose human-ity is, by definition, questionable); it is the mystery of the ex-haustive fulfillment of humanity at one point, one place, one time, and it is the mystery that, forever after, the divine and the human will exist in a relation of direct, not inverse proportion.

4.92 The other questions to be discussed are consequences of the teaching on the two natures of Jesus Christ. There is one which is of great interest and which is at the same time most problematic from the standpoint of the real humanity of Jesus. It is the question of the pre-existence of Jesus' person, or, in the more usual form, the question of his personal pre-existence.

Both parts of the expression *personal pre-existence* are unfortu-nate. As we have noted on more than one occasion, it is ex-tremely important to distinguish between the present-day mean-ing of the word *personal* ("pertaining to a distinct conscious subject") and its use when it translates a form or derivative of the Greek word *hypostasis* (roughly: "way of possessing exis-tence"). Furthermore, the word *pre*-existence assumes a tempo-ral relationship of eternity to time and commits the logical blunder of trying to define eternity in terms of temporal catego-ries. God does not really *pre-exist* anything; he simply exists in such a way that all else is derived from him. In eternity he exists *both* as one who is absolutely self-sufficient *and* as one who is totally committed to history. We can approach this mystery only by thinking of God (1) as the one who is absolutely alone in eternity and (2) as the one who eternally decides not to be alone. That is, we have to think of God in a way which would imply contradiction if the concepts were referred to any created thing. However, if our thought about God touches God in his reality (even if from an infinite distance), then God must really *be* this way. That is, there must be a real distinction in God between the absolutely independent and self-sufficient way in which he possesses his existence, and a second way in which he possesses this *same* existence—that is, as one who wills from all eternity to share his own life and his very self. Jesus Christ is the concrete shape and form which this eternal intent has taken in history.

Again, it is precisely at this point that we must underline the distinction between *personal* in the *modern* sense and *personal* in what might be called the *conciliar-theological sense,* where it is used to translate a form or a derivative of the Greek *hypostasis.* There are serious reasons for not speaking of the "personal pre-existence of Jesus Christ" when the word is used in the modern sense, but there are equally serious reasons for asserting the "personal pre-existence of Jesus Christ" when the word "personal" is used in the conciliar-theological sense, although it would seem better, because of the possible confusion, to use a more technical word such as "hypostatic pre-existence," which would pose less of a threat to the authentic humanity of Jesus. *Hypostatic pre-existence* would refer to the fact that God possesses his existence eternally in really distinct ways (three, to be exact, though only the first and second ways concern us here), and that the second way, called *Logos* or *Word,* has become historically real in Jesus. What this means is that in the *modern* sense of the word *person,* Jesus is the human person who is the perfect counterpart of God. In fact, it is his dialogue with the Father which is constitutive of his human personhood, in the modern sense of this latter word.[207]

Jesus is unique precisely because this unique dialogue with the Father makes him totally and exhaustively human, and not because of some element or factor in him which might compete with his humanity. If we use the word *person* in the modern sense (and, seriously, can we avoid doing this or should we try?), the denial of human personality in Jesus and the assertion of multiple personality in God does justice neither to the New Testament nor to the christological councils of the early Church. If the question is asked "What is there in Jesus which pre-exists his human conception?" then the answer must be: "That eternal distinction between God as incommunicable mystery and God as self-communicating mystery, to which we have alluded in this section." It is God as self-communicating mystery who is the ground of what is absolutely unique in Jesus: that as a human person (in the *modern* sense) he is the perfect counterpart and the very "otherness" of God. That the real God might be so totally committed to history was beyond the capacities of Greek categories of thought, but it is central to our faith.

It may be argued, I believe quite correctly, that since God and man are incommensurable, their real involvement with each other in history can be spoken of only in language which has strong mythological elements. Paul does this in taking up what was probably a pre-Pauline hymn in Philippians 2:5–11 and John does it at various points in his Gospel (many of them more impressive in this respect than the prologue). No one should find fault with mythological forms of expression, *provided they are recognized as such.* There is probably no other way in which we can speak of the absolute and the unconditioned. A sound program of demythologization does not seek to dispose of myth but rather to *decode* it (perhaps with the purpose of expressing its content in a new myth which would be more effective and less dangerous today). Myths cause problems and create dangers when they are not recognized for what they are, but are interpreted as the story of real personal encounters which preceded the world and time. If the pre-existence of Jesus' person were to be mythicized in this way, then it would pose a threat both to the human reality of Jesus and to the reality of God's commitment to history. The real mystery of our faith is not that of an eternal person (*modern* sense!) who might don human vesture and walk across the historical stage. The real mystery is that of a God who took time and history so seriously that he took into his very self the vulnerability of personal human encounter.

4.93 These remarks about the problems raised by the "pre-existence" of Jesus Christ make it possible to treat the question of *incarnation* more briefly. The term itself began as the Latin translation of a Greek abstract noun which ultimately went back to John 1:14: *Logos sarx egeneto*—usually translated "the Word became flesh." I would suggest that in view of the meaning of *sarx* in New Testament Greek (the created, human realm in its weakness and vulnerability),[208] this assertion in the prologue of John's Gospel should be regarded as an extremely exact theological statement of the meaning of the coming of Jesus. For the prologue, the essential assertion is not the coexistence of the word with God but the fact that "God was (the) Word" (Jn 1:1). This statement, so often used as a "proof text" in favor of the divinity of Christ, is not asserting something about the Word but about *God*—God is essentially one who goes outside himself and who chooses to be here. There is an infinite gap between God and the creature, but God, in his infinity, has bridged it. Because God eternally is Word, there will one day be a human being in whom God will take to himself all of the weakness and vulnerability of the human condition.

The concept of incarnation becomes problematic only when it is interpreted as the act in which a divine being (and a *person* in the modern sense) takes upon himself, or is immersed in, a human nature. This interpretation literalizes or historicizes the myth and refuses to see the coming of Jesus as the event in which God's commitment to history becomes real in an actual human person. Instead, it effectively isolates God from history, by treating history as a stage onto which the divine being might walk, as the framework within which he might act. Such a divine being would effectively escape that *becoming* which is intrinsic to, essential to history and thus satisfy an imperative of Greek thought. But such a "God," in refusing authentic historical involvement and engagement, does not satisfy the infinitely more important imperative of Christian thought. If the word *incarnation* is defined strictly within the limits imposed by a sound exegesis of the prologue of John's Gospel, it can be used without danger. The history of theology shows that it has not been defined this way and suggests that it be replaced with more directly scriptural locutions.

4.94 The next term of classical Christology which we will examine is far more technical: the term *hypostatic union* is not used by the earlier councils and is unknown even to a large number of rather well-informed Christians today. It has a place here because it has been accepted as the starting point of christological speculation up until the very recent past.[209] It is one of the most problematic of all the terms discussed here because it implies that the essential problem of Christology is that of *uniting* two distinct substances or natures in one person (*hypostasis*) and thus effectively calls into question the unity of Jesus Christ. But the real mystery of Jesus is not that of the union of disparate natures. The real mystery lies in the fact that in this concrete human person, *God(nt)* is present and God "happens." Not only is the union here not merely a moral one; *not even an ontological union* (that is, in which *principles of being* are involved) *is enough.* Nothing will do, short of the statement that *this man is the realization of God(nt).*

4.95 Another term which has caused problems is *kenosis*—(self-) emptying. It is derived from the famous text of Philippians 2:5–11 and it underwent considerable development in connection with the concept of pre-existence. It came to describe the fact that a pre-existent divine being had first to *lay aside* his divine prerogatives and power if he were to become human. As such the word is mythological, and the same remarks as were made about pre-existence apply here. Etymologically, of course, the word could be used to speak of the real participation of God in emptiness and nothingness by his entry into history through personal involvement with Jesus. However, the word remains a dangerous one because it implies that the real problem is that of explaining how an immutable God could have a changeable human nature as his own. There are many mysteries in theology, but this is not one of them. For this reason, I believe it would be better, both for faith and for the intelligent speculation which tries to serve faith, if this term, like "hypostatic union," were dropped from speculative Christology.

4.96   Finally, a word should be said about the question of the consciousness of Jesus. This was not a problem for conciliar and Scholastic Christology. It developed in step with the concern about the origins and character of human consciousness in general in the philosophy of the eighteenth and nineteenth centuries, and it led to the posing of two questions in Christology during the middle third of this century. First, since there are two natures in Christ, does he also possess two distinct consciousnesses? Second, to what degree are the contents of these consciousnesses to be kept separate? Specifically: Is Jesus as man (that is, in his human consciousness) aware of being God? How are we to conceive of such an awareness in itself and in its possibility of growth and development? As I noted earlier in this chapter the problem of the "two distinct consciousnesses" of Jesus is the type of question which was inspired by a certain understanding of the two-natures doctrine but which led in turn to an interpretation of that doctrine which represented a significant change in the doctrine itself. With reason, theology often avails itself of the terminology of technical or popular philosophy, but theologians are prone to forget that when, in a later age, these technical terms are inserted into a new and different context, they often undergo a considerable change in meaning.

It was in this way that the doctrine of the two natures, intelligible enough in the mid-fifth century, led finally to the absurd question of how the "contents" of Jesus' divine consciousness can be kept from "spilling over into" his human consciousness, so that those New Testament passages which speak of the limitations of Jesus' knowledge can be taken literally. Strangely enough, theologians rarely asked how real the human being was who could be faced with such problems. It is in the fact that it gave rise to such questions that the hidden dangers of the doctrine of the two natures became apparent. It is important for us all to be freed from such ways of speaking which make of Jesus Christ an ontological oddity, because otherwise we cannot be free for the real Jesus Christ—the man who is God's Son.

If we use the terms *consciousness* and *person* in the contemporary sense, we can say this: Jesus Christ is one human person, who, as such, is a knowing and loving subject. He knows himself as the counterpart of God, as the "other" who is known and loved by God in a way for which there is no analogy anywhere else. He knows and loves this Father, who is the "other" on whom his personhood depends. He grasps fully that he is of and from God and that in him the Father has found that "other" whom he has willed from all eternity to find. And Jesus knows all of this in his one human consciousness, his one developing act of awareness of self and awareness of the world around him. The real Jesus remains a mystery—the mystery of the absolutely transcendent God who has completely entered the worldly sphere through his dialogue with this man, and who, through the encounter with this man, has fashioned, as meeting persons always do, a new and mysterious domain—a realm of shared existence.

4.97 We can only begin to understand Jesus Christ from the place where we are now. This does not allow us to impose our modern interests and concerns on Jesus; on the contrary, it cautions us to be critical of these concerns and to strive to understand the limitations of our situation. When we reflect on our situation as Christians, particularly as this bears on the problem of Jesus Christ, we find that there are two factors which determine the character of this situation: first, we are called to be *hearers of the word,* to let the Jesus of the New Testament speak to us, and, second, this situation is determined by the fact that only a little more than a decade ago a sixteen hundred year old tradition in Catholic theology came to an end. So recent is this development that many in the Church are not even aware of it yet and others will spend much time and energy fighting it. But it will be in vain. The sixteen centuries during which Christology was dominated by Greek categories of thought—either in their original neo-Platonic form or in the later versions of Scholasticism and neo-Scholasticism—are over, but all of this has happened so recently that the way we ask questions and seek answers is still deeply marked by that epoch. We can turn to the New Testament and attempt to speak of the Jesus we find there only if we can be confident that we are not rejecting the substance of a tradition of faith which goes back to Nicaea. It has been the purpose of this chapter to show that we are not, and that the substance of the conciliar tradition can be maintained more effectively with the help of a conceptual system and a terminology very different from that of the early councils.

In this chapter we made no mention of the strange events which took place at the end of Jesus' earthly life. Reflection on these events did not have an important role to play at the councils which gave christological doctrine its definitive form, and therefore a contemporary reflection on these same questions did not belong to the work of this chapter. However, the events in question are those which have changed, once and for all, our relationship to God. In them the real meaning of Jesus is manifest. To show this is the work of the next chapter.

The Cross of Christ

For Paul and for Mark, the cross and the resurrection form the very substance of the good news, the "Gospel" which they preach. Cross and resurrection do this, not as two separated or separable events, but as two sides of the *same* event. Paul, for example, wants to preach only Jesus Christ, the crucified one (the Greek text makes it clear that this Jesus is and remains the crucified one),[210] but at the same time Paul knows that unless Christ rose from the dead, both his preaching and our faith are vain, empty, without content.[211] And Mark's Gospel has been described as a passion narrative with a long introduction. This is not a bad description, but it is obvious that such a passion narrative is worth writing only because its subject, Jesus, *lives*.

5.1 A Saving Event?

It is clear that for both Mark and Paul it is the death of Jesus Christ which achieved our salvation. But this conviction, so central to their writings, is, surprisingly, foreign to much of the New Testament, and apparently to many of the early Christian communities which were in existence before the writing of the New Testament. In fact, it is in that very Gospel, in which historical interest would seem to be most evident, that an interpretation of the cross as a saving event is lacking—in Luke's Gospel and in the Acts of the Apostles by the same author.[212] It is difficult to disagree with Ernst Käsemann's assertion that in Luke's writings the cross is simply a misunderstanding on the part of the Jews and therefore plays no essential role in the salvific work of Jesus Christ.[213]

There is evidence that Luke is not alone in being able to make nothing of the cross—in fact, before the time of Paul[214] and after that of Mark, practically no attempt was made in the New Testament to understand the cross and to interpret it as the event in which the salvation of all mankind was won.[215] In the sayings-source used by both Matthew and Luke (the Q document), there is not one single reference to the cross as a saving event.

It was obviously no easy matter to preach the cross in the Hellenistic communities, and the response which Paul encountered in Corinth makes this quite clear. The "Enthusiasts" there wanted to hear of nothing but the resurrection and the share in divine life which it brought them.[216] (Paul, in turn, reacted strongly against this "resurrection theology," and this dispute was the occasion of some of his most important statements on the meaning of the cross in 1 Corinthians 1 and 2.)

These "non-interpretations" of the cross in large parts of the New Testament are surprising enough, but critical scholarship has come to conclusions which would seem to be even bolder. The weight of solid exegetical opinion today does not support the authenticity of Jesus' so-called "predictions of the passion"—those statements in Mark 8:31 and the parallels where Jesus talks to his followers on the road to Caesarea Philippi and describes the final events of his life. The evidence is strong that this part of the Synoptic tradition is a Marcan construction which had its origin in the Easter events and the later preaching about these events.[217]

Faith has no reason to be fearful in the face of either of these assertions (the fact that Paul and Mark stand alone in regarding the cross as a saving event and the fact that Jesus' predictions of his suffering, death and resurrection are probably not authentic); there are other such constructions in the New

Testament, and there is too much disagreement in the New Testament even on essential matters to allow us to maintain the pretense of a single New Testament theology. But if facts and probabilities such as the ones mentioned pose no threat to faith, they certainly raise some interesting questions. Foremost among them is this: What does it mean to call the cross a saving event and *how did the cross achieve its effect*?

5.11 Although for Paul and Mark the cross is the central saving event, neither gives any obvious answer to the question of how the cross "worked" or why Jesus died. Neither tells us clearly what the death of this one man had to do with eternal life, or why God wanted it to happen that way. Both Paul and Mark seem content to assert that by his death Jesus saved us or redeemed us[218] or won a victory over the "powers."[219] A number of texts speak of the death of Jesus in a terminology reminiscent of that of the Old Testament sacrificial worship. His death is seen, for example, as the act through which God renewed his covenant[220] or as a renewal of the sacrifice of the pasch.[221] When Paul seems to be speaking directly about the cross (in Romans 3:21–26) he makes use of both legal and cultic terms which led some later interpreters to find in these passages the essence of Anselm's satisfaction theory (see below). But the best exegesis of these passages indicates that Paul is making use of juridical and cultic language to affirm that what the sacrificial worship of the Old Testament *sought* to achieve was actually accomplished in and through the death of Jesus Christ—namely, *the reconciliation of man with God* and *not the reconciliation of God with man.* It is totally foreign to Paul's thought to think of God as one who would placate himself through the work of Jesus or who would arrange to have himself placated in this way. Nothing illustrates this fact more clearly than Paul's capsule summary of the meaning of the cross in 2 Corinthians 5:19: "God was in him reconciling the world to himself."

However, even here there is no obvious answer to the
question of why Jesus died and of how his death achieved its
saving effects even on human beings who would live long after
the death of the Lord. Even Paul's longer treatment of the cross
in 1 Corinthians 1 and 2 gives us no evident interpretation of
the event (although I am convinced that a careful exegesis of
these texts can bring to light his understanding of the cross).

5.12 As a result of the absence of clear-cut interpretations of
the cross in Paul and Mark, the field was left open for later
theologians to develop many theories to explain how the cross
"worked," how it achieved its saving effects. In general, such
theories have been distinguished more for their ingenuity and
subtlety than for their dependence on the New Testament and
they tell us more about the philosophical and cultural traditions
in vigor at different periods of Church history than they do
about the real meaning of the death of the Lord.

5.13 The Greek patristic period offered a variety of interpretations. Of these, the most enduring and least dangerous was the
notion that the cross was in some way the fulfillment of the
incarnation, in that it showed the full and unreserved entry of
God into the human condition. For such a theory it is really the
incarnation which is the saving event, because it is there that
human nature is touched by divine nature. The philosophical
tradition since Plato made it easy and natural for the Fathers of
the Eastern Church to think of human nature as something
common, really shared by all human beings with Jesus Christ and
which, as such, could be touched by the divine nature with which
it coexisted in him. For such a theory the cross itself is not really
the saving event; rather, it has the function of demonstrating
that Jesus is really human and that he participated in every
situation which human nature normally faces. The theory was
strong in emphasizing the solidarity of Jesus with the rest of the

human race and the solidarity of God with us through him, but it based this solidarity on an inadequate anthropology and in the final analysis it was unable to do justice to the Pauline thesis of the saving significance of the death of the Lord. (But this was the fate of all of the characteristic theses of Paul's theology during the patristic period. What was distinctive in Paul's thought virtually disappeared from view before the end of the first century and has reappeared even sporadically only at those times when the hold of Greek patterns of thought has weakened and men have become open once more to the paradox of a God who is involved with space and time and the brokenness of man.)

5.14 Other theories which enjoyed currency during the patristic period were quite strange. Some argued that the devil had been tricked into overreaching himself by arranging for the death of the Son of God. According to this view, the divinity of Christ was a carefully guarded secret (this was Origen's explanation of the messianic secret!) and the devil was prevented from knowing it, in order to entice him to conspire in the death of Jesus (who was obviously, even to the devil, a man of God). The devil fell into the trap and dared to raise a hand against Jesus, who was, unknown to him, the Son of God. As a result of this (unintended!) arrogance, the devil lost power not only over Jesus; he also lost the power he had been given over all other human beings at the time of the fall of our first parents, Adam and Eve.

Still another theory which was popular for a time was that which took the notion of *redemption* (buying back) very literally, and asked from whom we were bought when Jesus paid his death as a price. Some argued that it was God to whom the price was paid, while others argued that the devil was bought off and that as a result he had released men from their bondage to him. These theories enjoyed only a limited popularity, even in the

East, and they do not have to be taken seriously as attempts at theological understanding. They have always enjoyed a certain popularity in preaching and some devotional works, and here their harmfulness has continued almost up to the present day.

5.15   In the Western empire, no single explanation of the saving significance of Jesus' death dominated the field. It was common enough to assert that Jesus *substituted* himself for us, but little was said about why this was necessary or how it was possible. Ambrose and Hilary of Poitiers speak of the death of the Lord as an act of *restitution* or *satisfaction,* but they say nothing about why such an act was needed or how the death of this one man constituted such an act of satisfaction. It was not until the time of Anselm of Canterbury (died 1109) that this explanation was worked out with logical consistency and stated with such clarity that it dominated thought on the death of Jesus Christ almost up to the present day.

5.2   The Anselmian Satisfaction Theory

The theory under discussion here has done enormous harm, not only on the theoretical level, but in very practical matters which touch the individual and the community, the spirituality of each member of the Church and the worship of the Church at large. Juan Alfaro, who wrote the section on Anselm's theory for the original German edition of *Mysterium Salutis,*[222] gives a good summary. The following is an English translation of the relevant section of his article.

> Anselm of Canterbury developed . . . a new conception
> of salvation which was based on God's right to his
> honor. Sin is an injury to and a personal insult offered
> to the honor of God. God cannot ignore the demands
> of his honor and therefore he must demand restitution

for the insult done to him. From this results the dilemma: either sinful humanity makes restitution for the infinite insult offered to God, or it will be punished. Either the honor of which God was deprived is restored to him or God will demand the punishment due. Sinful man could not make restitution for the injury; only the Son of God could, after his incarnation, offer satisfaction by means of his death—a satisfaction which corresponds to the magnitude of the insult. (His love and obedience would not be enough, because acts of these virtues are due God independently of the sin of man.) For this reason the incarnation was absolutely necessary because it was the only way of making restitution to the divine honor and was therefore ineluctably demanded by this honor.[223]

5.21 Anselm's theory was reworked by Thomas Aquinas and was stripped of some of its more crudely juridical and mythological elements, but the structure of the theory was untouched and in that form it has held a place of honor in the dogma manuals practically up to the present day. From that position it has continued to exercise a devastating influence on prayer, asceticism and popular piety.

5.22 The worst thing about Anselm's theory is the picture of God which stands behind it. God is one who, like a feudal lord, insists on a *quid pro quo* return of honor for insult received. He must demand restitution, and in the final analysis he is the one *acted upon* by having these demands of his met, and by receiving proportionate satisfaction. Anselm, of course, felt that God arranged for things to happen this way, and he assumed (and asserted) that God was the ultimate cause of the whole process, but this results in an ever stranger picture: the divine actor is somehow constrained by his very nature to demand satisfaction or forced into playing a kind of game in which his justice is delicately balanced against his mercy. The most negative aspect of Anselm's theory is the theological sadism it presupposes: God is pleased by suffering and punishment and is really indifferent as to whether it strikes the innocent or the guilty. (Thomas mitigated precisely this aspect of Anselm's theory but was then unable to say anything convincing about the relationship of death to salvation.)

5.23   The view of God implied by this theory has been propagated in countless sermons and manuals of piety and devotion. Time and time again we have heard variations on this theme: God is the one who must be propitiated or appeased and we must make atonement to him for our sins. The picture is that of a powerful lord who must be placated and thus reconciled to us. He is pictured as one who is ready to strike unless an appropriate peace-offering is made and who is prevented from exacting a terrible vengeance only by the fact that his Son, Jesus Christ, "gets in the way" and absorbs the divine wrath which was directed toward us.

In this connection, it is interesting to note that many Catholic exegetes, even in the recent past, felt duty-bound to make room for the Anselmian theory of satisfaction by interpreting Paul's term *dikaiosune* as the justice of God which demands satisfaction and compensation for the evil of sin and for the deprivation of divine glory which was brought about by man's rebellion. Huby, for example, affirms that *dikaiosune* is the just and merciful action of God who obtained satisfaction for sins through the sacrifice of the cross. . . ."[224] Schelkle affirms that *dikaiosune* ". . . reveals God's justice, in that atonement for sin is demanded on the cross."[225] Even Otto Kuss speaks ambiguously here and asserts that *dikaiosune* includes "the demanding holiness of God which makes the frightful death on the cross 'necessary.' " Kuss is convinced that there is an element in Paul's theology which is not adequately covered by such concepts as love, mercy and forgiveness (*and in this he is right*). However then he asserts that this element is God's demand that justice be fulfilled by the suffering of Christ, but there is nothing *in his own exegesis of the passage* (Rom 3:21–26) that supports this interpretation.

Anselm's theory in all of its forms makes God the *object* of reconciliation and is thus very far from the fundamental assertion of Paul which was cited above: "God was in Christ, reconciling the world to himself" (2 Cor 5:19). For Paul, God is the *subject* of reconciliation, the one who *does* it.

5.24 This point is so important that it is worth while pausing briefly here to examine that Pauline text which has so often been invoked in support of Anselm's theory—the text of Romans 3:25 in which Paul talks about Christ "whom God publicly manifested as a means of atonement." The key word here is *hilasterion,* the Greek word which I have translated as "means of atonement." This has often been used by proponents of the satisfaction theory to show that God sent Jesus to his death so that he (God) might be appeased and his justice satisfied, but the text itself does not support this interpretation. Three points will make this clear. First, Paul is almost certainly using a formula of the Jewish-Christian community here. The rarity of the term in his own writings (coupled with his own conviction of the centrality of the death of the Lord) is otherwise inexplicable. Second, the word *may* have referred to the cover of the tabernacle in the Holy of Holies and therefore to the place where God was thought to be present and accessible in a special way on the day of atonement; but the translation given above is simpler and would include this. Third, in any case, Paul is using a Jewish-Christian *theologoumenon* (theological conception) as a way of stating that God is the *author* and *subject* of the atoning act and not its recipient and object.

5.3   The Death of the Lord in the New Testament: Paul's Teaching

A reputable theology of the cross has to begin with the New Testament. The various attempts of the patristic period and of the early and late Scholastic periods to come to terms with the salvific meaning of the death of Jesus do not pass this test, and it is time to turn now to the two New Testament writers for whom the cross is the heart of the matter—Paul and Mark. Neither gives us a very obvious theology of the cross, but if the distorting lens of the Anselmian satisfaction theory is laid aside, I believe that a cogent statement of the meaning of the suffering and death of the Lord can be derived from their writings.

5.31   For Paul the cross is the center of all theology, the ground of faith, and the means of our justification. Paul wants to know "only Jesus Christ, the crucified one,"[226] and there is only one thing he really wants and that is to "boast only of the cross of our Lord Jesus Christ."[227] He declares that "we proclaim Christ crucified—to the Jews a scandal and to the Gentiles foolishness, but to those who have been called, Jews and Gentiles alike, the wisdom and power of God."[228]

Paul's theology not only includes a theological interpretation of the cross; it *is* a theology of the cross. This is evident not only from Paul's words about the cross itself; paradoxically, it is when he speaks of the incarnation and the resurrection that he offers even more convincing proof that for him the cross is the heart of the matter. In the powerful cadences of Romans 8:38–39 Paul states that he is "convinced that nothing in heaven or on earth . . . can separate us from the love of God which he has shown in Jesus Christ." But this text in no way shifts the center of gravity from the cross to the incarnation or to the public life of Jesus, and the verses which immediately precede those cited make this clear: the God who has shown his love is the one "who did not spare his own Son but handed him over for us."[229] Obviously Paul knows of the incarnation, but the theory so dear to the Platonizing Fathers of the Eastern Church from Irenaeus to John of Damascus—the theory that the union of divine and human natures in the Word had, of itself, elevated human nature to a share in divinity—was unknown to Paul. Christ incarnate saves, but only as the man who came to die on the cross.

The same is true of the resurrection. No writer in the New Testament took the resurrection more seriously than Paul: he told the Corinthians that "if Christ was not raised, then both our preaching and your faith are in vain."[230] But Paul knew that in the ancient world there was no dearth of men or of heroes who had been brought back to life by the power of the gods. And for Paul, the resurrected Christ is always the Christ who died for our sins. Greece, in both its ancient and its Hellenistic periods, knew of dying and rising gods; however, it never knew of a death which was not canceled or relativized by resurrection, but, on the contrary, endowed with permanent meaning. This paradox belongs to the Christian message alone, and whenever this message is preached, it owes much of its authority and power to Paul of Tarsus, for whom the good news was simply "the word of the cross."

When Paul tried to answer the question of why the cross had such saving power, he often used imagery which is quite foreign to us today. But overriding all of the legal and cultic metaphors and relativizing all of them is a single truth of absolute importance: on the cross it is God himself who acts to bring man's estrangement to an end: "God was in Christ reconciling the world to himself."[231] If there is a single sentence which sums up all of Paul's thought, this is it. Every word is important: God is not compensated for injuries received, nor is he offered the suffering of an innocent man to induce him to refrain from punishing the guilty. On the contrary, "he shows his love for us in that Christ died for us while we were still sinners."[232] Unfortunately, the famous text of Romans 3:25 has so often been invoked in favor of Anselm's satisfaction theory that even the translations often speak of Christ as a "sacrificial offering" or a "propitiation." However, as I noted earlier in this chapter, this text does not speak of a sacrifice which God arranged to satisfy his justice, but rather of the act through which God himself restores the broken covenant. It is through the death of Jesus that God makes a new covenant in which men are to share by faith.[233]

5.32   For Paul, because the cross is first and foremost God's act, it is the event in which God is revealed as the one who wants reconciliation. It is this insight which makes it possible to define God's relationship to sinful human beings while not at the same time creating a "god" who is a demonic parody of human vindictiveness. The "justice" which God "makes manifest on the cross"[234] is unique in that, through it, we are "made just, in virtue of his loving kindness, as a free gift."[235] His justice, as he himself defines it, seeks neither appeasement nor satisfaction nor punishment; his justice is a synonym for the unconditioned love and acceptance with which he claims the sinner as his own. Paul's words still echo the wonder of one who has grasped and been grasped by the good news: "What will we say to this? If God is for us, who is against us? If he did not spare his own Son but gave him over on behalf of us, is it not true that with him he has given us every gift?"[236] This is the first element of Paul's theology of the cross: the cross is the revelation of the paradoxical justice of God.

But how does the cross reveal this paradoxical justice of God? This brings us to the second element of Paul's theology of the cross: the cross reveals God's justice because in and through the death of Jesus God effectively *redefines* man. On the cross, God reconciles us by making real in time and in history the truth about man. On the cross God reveals what it means to be human, and this revelation is both a judgment on man's understanding of himself and a rejection of it. Man on his own is fascinated by his own autonomy. He prizes his "wisdom" because it enables him to use the world and those who are in it in order to assert himself. He prizes his "strength" because it gives him the power to dominate his world, to impose his will on others and to make them serve him. Hypnotized by his own "wisdom" and "strength," man defines himself as one who achieves success and fulfillment in giving free rein to his self-assertive and self-aggrandizing drives.

On the cross God rejects this definition and shows that "the foolishness of God is wiser than the wisdom of men."[237] For the man who relies only on his own strength, lowliness can inspire only contempt and the threat of lowliness can inspire only fear. But in the death of Jesus, God becomes implicated in the ultimate lowliness of death, and because of this the deeper meaning of lowliness and death is revealed: they are not obstacles in the way of our self-fulfillment but ways in which we may come to understand and accept the deepest truth of the human situation. The real human being is not one who dominates but one who serves, not one who "grasps at equality with God" but one who "shares the existence of a slave."[238] We are truly human, not when we play at being God, but when we accept our own creaturehood. This is the "word of the cross" which is "the power of God for those who are to be saved."[239] The ultimate lowliness of death is no longer the final tragedy; it is the way of accepting and affirming our real selves before God; it is acceptance of the truth and therefore, at the deepest level, an act of faith.

In the mythical language of the third chapter of Genesis, sin had come into the world because men would be like God. Unwilling to accept their status as creatures, they aspired to greatness and ultimacy. But on the cross God shows what it

means to be a creature.[240] There, Jesus was stripped of everything
which impressed his followers as superhuman in power and
messianic in significance. At that moment his existence was that
of a slave—unprotected and vulnerable. His human wisdom was
no more and his human strength was broken, and he died with a
cry of abandonment on his lips. Man is a creature, and to show
what this means God shares in death through the death of his
Son.

Yet if man is willing to be nothing but a creature, by the
same token he is willing to let God be nothing but Creator, and
this is the third main element in Paul's theology of the cross.
When man accepts the nothingness of his own being, as this is
fully and finally manifest in death, then he allows God to be
really God and to be the Creator who "brings the dead to life
and calls into being the things that are not."[241] On the cross
God defines man as creature not in order to crush and destroy
him; God defines man as creature so that he may be with man as
nothing but Creator. If man depends on himself, then he has
everything to fear and his anxiety will eventually destroy him.
On the other hand, if he depends on God, then he has nothing
to fear and it is the death of Jesus which made this evident. Jesus
made no claims for himself and died as a slave, the most despised of men. But it was then, precisely then, that God manifested himself as Creator and "raised him from the dead and
gave him the name which is above every other name."[242]

The cross is not the tragic story of a man who died almost
two millennia ago. The cross is a call *now* to accept the definition
of God and the definition of ourselves which Jesus enacted and
made real in and through his death. The cross is a call to pass
judgment on ourselves and on our ideas of strength and of
wisdom and to accept the strange paradox that "the foolishness
of God is wiser than the wisdom of men." Paul's powerful
parallelism simply reaffirms the original paradox of Jesus' own

teaching: "He who saves his life will lose it; he who loses it for my sake will save it."[243]

In Paul's view, the cross changes the meaning of the whole situation of man, but Paul talks about this in idioms which are, at first sight, quite strange to us: he affirms that on the cross Christ freed us from sin, from death and from the law. Paul knew, of course, that none of these had come to an end as such; they were still factors in human life and they could be disruptive enough, but their power to work definitive harm was forever broken. Sin, death and the law can no longer crush man, because in one man, Jesus Christ, they were relativized and rejected.

When Paul talks about Christ's conquest of sin, he is not thinking primarily of the forgiveness of sin or sins. In Paul's view, sin is not the violation of a law or a commandment, or even the refusal to do the will of God. Sin is not really a transgression but a *situation,* in which man does not know and trust God and is therefore not at peace with the world or with himself. It is a situation in which man refuses to know God and therefore misuses the world and himself. It is a tragic situation in which man is alienated from the only one who can give him security, joy and peace. And it is a situation in which man tries desperately to provide himself with security and fails.

We long to live, but we live in terror of an end which comes inexorably. In one respect death is, for us as for all other living things, a natural event and a part of life itself. But we cannot accept it as the other animals do; instead, we are appalled by its approach and we resist it as though it were an unnatural affront to our spiritual being. In the face of death we experience the radical insecurity which is our permanent companion during life, and, as always, we hide from it—usually by striving to find some quality or some achievement of our own which holds the promise of permanence and stability—something of which we

can "boast." It is this attempt which drives us to *use* others and
to make them objects of our control and victims of our power.
To act this way is to despise others and ourselves as well, and in
doing it we become, as Paul says in the great text of Romans
1:19–31, ". . . unloving and unpitying. . . ." The final tragedy is
that in making use of others we lose the power to have any real
love and pity for ourselves.

What we need to escape from this situation of sin is *faith:*
total reliance on God. But we are fearful of doing this—fearful
that if we do not watch out for ourselves, no one will, aware that
if we place our trust in another, our own power and wisdom will
count for nothing. We have all tasted power and we prefer it to
faith. This is the point that Paul saw so clearly in Romans 3:27
when he asked "Do we have anything to boast about?" and
answered, "Nothing at all!" If God recognized our claims on
him because of our observance of law, then we would have a fine
way of securing ourselves against God. This is not only the
temptation of Paul's Jewish contemporaries; it is the permanent
temptation of "religious" man, who wants moral, religious and
ceremonial laws to secure himself against God. Paul's gospel,
like the Gospel of Mark, is an attack against "religious" man in
this sense, and Paul's teaching that God gives us a claim on him
through faith alone is directed against that religiosity which is a
permanent human temptation. This sheds a good deal of light
on Paul's view that sin actually makes use of the law in order to
intensify man's estrangement from God.

The situation of sin shows that God's eternal will to find
another who would be his counterpart had never found a commensurate response. Man's usual response to God was rebellion
and, at best, he might arrange a kind of pact with God which
could be regulated by law—an arrangement in which man allot-
ted God "his place" and served him there; an arrangement in
which human beings were servants, but not friends, and certainly not sons and daughters. But God's will to find a counterpart

did not fail, and one day the human being came who would hear the call and who would be the fulfillment in time of God's eternal will to find a Son. However the paradox of the situation is that this one who is his Son belongs to a race and a world which are alienated from God. This one who is his Son shares the body, the history, the life of an estranged world, and in this paradox lie the tragedy and the glory of the cross.

5.33 Paul has a good deal to say, directly and by implication, about man under the judgment of the cross, and this will be the occasion here of some final remarks about the cross and religious law. Paul's solemn programmatic statement here should never be forgotten: "Christ is the end of the law."[244] This must have been a hard judgment for the converted Jewish scholar, but Paul had come to the conclusion that although the law commanded many things that were good, it contained within itself the most dangerous of all temptations, the most disruptive of all man's attempts to win autonomy: the religious illusion that he can, by his own efforts, bridge the chasm which separates him from God. Paul's polemic was directed in actual fact against the law of Moses, but his attack is valid against any and every moral and religious system which caters to man's inborn desire to claim a hold on God on the basis of his own strength and wisdom and piety. When Paul asserts that the cross has freed men from the curse of the law, he means that through the death of Christ we are freed from the illusions of our own religiosity. The death of Christ on the cross was calculated from the beginning to call religious tradition into question, because religious traditions tend to be institutionalized expressions of our convictions of how God should act. The cross is nothing less than an affront to man's own view of where God is to be found, and for this reason it is precisely in respect to man's religious convictions and expectations that the cross is "foolishness and a scandal."[245]

Man insists on making God in his own image and likeness, and this "god," like man himself, has no use for the lowliness of the cross. The real God does. He judges and rejects man's definition of the word "God" and by implication he rejects man's definition of himself. The cross allows us to be ourselves and frees us from the need to play God and to cultivate the pretense that ultimate meaning is the work of our own hands. Under the cross we come to a new understanding of ourselves. We are freed from delusions of grandeur and made free for service in the real world. God reconciles our world to himself by revealing himself to the world and the world to itself.

But to be effective, revelation must be received, because only then does it function as an active and transforming force in our lives. This is a central point in Paul's theology of the cross: God's revelation is complete when man accepts the truth about God and about himself. The cross is an act of covenant-renewing reconciliation which is "to be taken advantage of through faith." Such faith is simply the willingness to accept God's gift— an act which undercuts man's pretensions to autonomy. Faith is the acceptance of the new definitions of God and man which were made on the cross.

In this section it has been evident that Paul has spoken about the cross, using a conceptual framework and imagery which are quite foreign to us. He was so convinced that the cross is the heart of the matter that he never tired of devising new ways to speak of the only Jesus Christ he knew: the crucified Lord. He tried to speak of the cross in ever new accents because he knew that "the word of the cross is the power of God."[246] As we leave this brief discussion of Paul's theology of the cross, it will be good to emphasize again that the cross is God's work, in and through Jesus. God reconciles man by revealing who man is; however, this revelation does not consist in the communication of theoretical truths but in a lived human life in which man's pseudo-values are overturned. Since this false scale of values is synonymous with sin, is confirmed by the law and is sealed by death, the death of Jesus Christ marks the end of the period in which these three destructive powers hold sway. When God gave to Jesus "a name which is above every other name"[247] he validated forever this new interpretation of lowliness and death. To call Jesus "Lord" is to accept this message about who the real God is and who the real human being is. It is to accept a God who is really Creator and a man who is really creature—and therefore it is to accept freedom and peace.

5.4 The Death of the Lord in Mark

In writing a Gospel, Mark invented a new literary form, and it is certainly no exaggeration to call his Gospel a major theological achievement. Paul gave us a very profiled theology of the cross, but almost no information about the life of Jesus, and for this reason he leaves us with a question: Is Paul's interpretation of Jesus' death supported by Jesus' own preaching? For a number of reasons, Mark is the most likely place to look for an answer to this question.

There is much truth in Schlatter's famous description of Mark's Gospel as a passion narrative with a long introduction, and this fact implies that everything in the "long introduction" must be examined with care if we want to discover Mark's theology of the cross. It is, strangely enough, in those parts of the Gospel which are probably not historical (that is, in those parts which are Marcan constructions) that we find material which sheds light both on Mark's view of the cross and on those elements in Jesus' own life and ministry on which this view was based. It is in such passages that Mark interpreted for a generation which had never known Jesus during his earthly life the meaning of certain characteristics of Jesus' message which were rooted in the life and ministry of Jesus of Nazareth. The much-discussed "messianic secret" is a case in point. According to

Mark, Jesus often accompanied his miracles with the command to say and do nothing to publicize them. (Sometimes the command is addressed to the demons, as in 1:25 and 1:34, and at other times to the person cured or healed, as in 1:40–45.) Eduard Schweizer interprets this strange secrecy of Jesus in a way that confirms what we have already found in Paul: it is the cross which reveals who God and man really are.

> Mark's answer is that the time for proclamation has not come, since the secret of Jesus will become really apparent only on the cross and one must follow him on the way of the cross to be able to really understand it. For this reason, the proclamation of the demons, the healed, and even the disciples, however exact it may be, can only do harm until Jesus' path to the cross makes it possible for men to follow him and even makes that following an irrevocable requirement.[248]

The messianic secret is almost certainly a Marcan construction, but it seems to be an interpretation of a fact which critical scholarship interprets almost unanimously as historical: Jesus' own extreme reserve in regard to the title of Christ or Messiah. At the time the Gospels were written, the Christian community had been confessing Jesus as Messiah for some time; in the light of the fact that on other occasions the community read its faith back into the story of Jesus, why was such restraint shown here? The only answer can be that within the community, at least when Mark wrote, there was still a living memory of the man Jesus, who, while claiming to speak and act in the name of God himself, had understood his mission in a way to which the traditional title of "Messiah" could not do justice. The word "Messiah" would be serviceable only after it was defined in a new way, and it was redefined on the cross.

It is another Marcan construction which makes this clear:

the first prediction of the passion.[249] Mark places the scene near Caesarea Philippi and has Jesus turn to the apostles and ask, "Who do people say that I am?" When Peter finally answers, "You are the Messiah," Jesus immediately orders his followers to tell no one about this and begins to explain that "the Son of Man must suffer much, and be rejected . . . and . . . be put to death." The import of this story is clear: Jesus would be Messiah only on his own terms. The definition of the word "Messiah" which was current in Jesus' own day would be harmful as a description, and the word could be used only after Jesus had given it a new meaning on the cross. For Mark, Jesus' whole public life is lived under the sign of the cross, and his death is simply the culmination of his life and preaching. Jesus dies on unconsecrated ground, outside the walls of the holy city, but during his life he had already broken down the walls which men had raised between the sacred and the profane realms. In dying he experienced the depths of abandonment, but in life he had been constantly misunderstood by his own followers and they all deserted him before the end. A "God" masquerading in human form could never make the fate of the man on the cross his very own, but in life Jesus had revealed God with an unheard of directness and immediacy, precisely in his totally human engagement on behalf of the world's weak and despised. Mark gives us his theology of the cross in showing the continuity of Jesus' life and death, and his *interpretation* of Jesus is transparent to certain characteristics of Jesus of Nazareth which are historically beyond question.

Central to Mark's Gospel is the conviction that Jesus reveals who the real God is. In the first chapter of the Gospel, Jesus preaches "the good news of God: the right time has come and God's rule is near."[250] But the rule of God is not something for the future; it is already present in Jesus. We can understand what Mark means by this if we keep in mind an interesting fact that historical-critical study of the Gospel has brought to light:

apart from the passion narrative, the actions and events of Jesus' life are given in an order which has nothing to do with the sequence of the events themselves but is rather the creation of Mark. As a result, Mark's arrangement of the events tells us a good deal about the way he understood Jesus and his message. If Mark's interpretation coincides in its essentials with Paul's and if Mark's interpretation stands in continuity with Jesus' own life and preaching, then we have excellent evidence for anchoring Paul's theology of the cross in the historical reality of Jesus of Nazareth.

According to Mark, Jesus reveals the unconditioned mercy of God; this is clear from the way in which Mark tells his story in the second chapter of the Gospel. The chapter begins with the story of the paralyzed man who is privileged to hear the words, "My son, your sins are forgiven." The story is often understood as a tale of divine omniscience and forgiveness, at the end of which even the teachers of the law unknowingly bear witness to the divinity of Christ with the remark: "No man can forgive sins; only God can."[251] But this misses tbe whole point of the Marcan arrangement. Mark's purpose is not to show that Jesus is God, as though his hearers already knew what the word "God" meant and simply had to learn to apply its contents to Jesus. Rather the point is just the opposite: it is Jesus who, by his words and actions, will show who the real God is.[252]

The remark made by the teachers of the law really prepares the way for the next story Mark recounts: immediately after Jesus quite consciously acts in God's name and God's own person, Mark shows him eating with sinners and tax collectors, much to the annoyance of the scribes and the Pharisees. Mark 2:13–17 is a commentary on Mark 2:1–12 and shows that the first story (the forgiveness of the sins of the paralyzed man) has nothing to do with an easy-going tolerance on the part of God, or with his recognition of man's basic good will. The publicans and sinners of Mark 2:13–17 are precisely that—*sinners*—and there is no attempt in the Gospels to suggest that their sins were not serious and real. But when Jesus shares a meal with them, he acts as though they are brought into the presence of the one in whose name he acts—God. In this event, God is with them and God accepts them without any prior conditions. No wonder they felt at ease in his presence: *the word "God" has been given a new meaning.*

This new definition of God is not a religious one. Religious man knows how to please his God by acts of piety, by correct ceremony and by orthodox faith, and he feels secure in the acceptance of God, which he has merited and won. But in the story of Mark 2:13–17 Jesus effects and makes real the acceptance of God precisely on behalf of that group which is without religious credentials and has nothing on which to base a claim on God. As if this were not enough, Mark underlines the point in the following story (2:18–22). Some people had asked Jesus why the Pharisees and the followers of John the Baptist fasted, while his own disciples did not. Jesus answered with a question: "Do you expect the guests at a wedding feast to go without food?" The point of the question is this: the final age has dawned and God is definitively present here and now. And God shows himself, in Jesus, as one who is not interested in religious performance and ascetical achievement. (There is some indication that verse 20 was added to the text at a time when the Church had reintroduced the practice of fasting.)[253]

All these stories show one thing: in Jesus, men encountered God in a way that brought them a new understanding of themselves and new freedom. Inevitably, this brought Jesus into conflict with the great religious and ethical norm of his own people: the law. For Mark, as for Paul, Jesus brings freedom from the law and not from the Jewish law alone.

Man's attitude toward the law is quite ambivalent. Although he suffers under the imposition of law, in a deeper sense he actually welcomes it, for obedience to the law gives him a claim, based on an admirable quality of his very own, which he can maintain against God himself. Man is not content to rely totally on God and to let everything rest on God's mercy and forgiveness; he insists that his own goodness be effective in removing the barriers that separate him from God. And it is in precisely this sense that Christ is the end of the law. Mark 2:13–17 and the parallel passages in the other evangelists which speak of Jesus as one who shared meals with outcasts and sinners show him as *one who rejected in principle the notion that the law and its prohibitions can actually separate good people from sinners and the notion that by obeying ethical and religious prescriptions one can do one's part in achieving salvation.*

The evidence is strong that in these and similar texts we are not dealing with constructions of the early Christian community, but with stances taken by Jesus himself. The little parable of the self-growing seed in Mark 4:26–29 asserts that the "kingdom" comes to man independently of his ethical and religious attempts at self-salvation. This is the only one of the parables of Mark which does not appear in any form in the other Gospels; apparently the community did not know what to make of this message (or was embarrassed by it!) even as the New Testament was being written. But communities do not invent stories which they find incomprehensible or embarrassing.

A similar point could be made in respect to the story recounted in Mark 7:1–23. The issue is a typically religious one: the disciples of Jesus are apparently violating one of God's regulations by eating with ritually unwashed hands, and the Pharisees notice this and complain about it. The heart of Jesus' answer is contained in 7:14–15: "Listen to me, all of you, and understand. There is nothing that goes into a person from the outside that can make him unclean." What we have here is nothing short of a programmatic rejection of a "God" who is pleased by conformity to ritual requirements and of religious man who revels in a law which prescribes perfectly clear religious duties. This story has been interpreted in a trivial way at times, as though Jesus were rejecting a religion of the letter in the name of a religion of the spirit, but his criticism goes much deeper. Jesus offers man freedom, not primarily from some antiquated religious nonsense but from his need to achieve religious security by being able to point to his own piety.

What is interesting in this story is that, like the others in which Jesus seems to reject the ground rules of religious behavior, it is a story which radical historical criticism sees as rooted in historically indisputable characteristics of Jesus himself.[254] What we have, therefore, is a new definition of both God and man, given not by Mark, but by Jesus. The revolutionary attack on the law and tradition which the Pharisees quite correctly see in Jesus' teaching consists in the fact that Jesus makes the real God present, a God whom no one really knew, and this means nothing less than the end of an old world and the beginning of a new one. In Jesus, God is at work, judging and rejecting man's idea of what he (God) must be like, what he must do, how he must act, what is appropriate for him. In the encounter with Jesus, human beings can learn to accept God on his own terms, to find him where he wishes to be found and not where we prefer to find him.

For Mark, the encounter which teaches this lesson in an unsurpassable way is the cross. Eduard Schweizer's comment on the first prediction of the passion is excellent on this point:

> God is God in as much as he can do what man cannot: he can permit himself to be rejected, to be lowly and insignificant. Man would be plunged into the depths of an inferiority complex, and this would show that what man wants with all his heart is to be great. Whoever understands the suffering of the Son of God has understood God. It is here and not in heavenly glory that he sees the heart of God.[255]

Schweizer makes the same point in his commentary on Mk 15:32 ("Let him come down from the cross and then we will believe"):

> This is how God differs from any man or superman— he does not have to assert himself, nor is it necessary for him to prove that he is right or to crush his enemies. This is the message of Jesus' passion.[256]

5.5 The Death of the Lord: A Contemporary Statement

Mark and Paul have really spoken with one voice: the death of Jesus is the revelation of God. God is manifest in obscurity and disgrace and lowliness. Jesus has lived out to the very end his own words in Mark 8:35: "The man who wants to save his own life will lose it, but the man who loses his life for the Gospel will save it." If one attempts to make his own life secure, if one strives for an illusory greatness by using others and forcing them to serve him, if one plays God in his own small corner of the world, then such a one "loses his life," foregoes the real and authentic existence which God alone can offer. But if one is willing to be a creature and to accept the brokenness, fragility and failure that characterize the human condition, then such a one will "save his life" because in giving up his pretensions he allows God to be God, to be the one "who calls into being the things that are not and raises the dead to life."[257]

The time has come now to draw on the scriptural evidence and to attempt the task of saying in our words today what Paul and Mark said in their words then.

5.51 The cross is the central mystery of faith, but like all mysteries it begins by making two demands on us. First, mystery demands that we be clear about just what the mystery consists in, precisely where it is. Mystery is not nonsense and it is not contradiction. It is not offered to us to frustrate our intelligence or to mortify our minds. If we are asked to sacrifice our intelligence, then we can be certain that what confronts us is not mystery, but rather some philosophical *tour de force* which can lay no proper claim to our allegiance as Christians. The second claim that mystery makes on us is that we see in it not a purely theoretical truth that is designed to titillate, if not frustrate the intelligence, but rather a most practical truth, the acceptance of which is nothing less than the willingness to undergo a total transformation. Mysteries are not the truths which we cannot understand, but they are certainly truths which we understand in a radically different way. A mystery is not an object which we could fix with a gaze and about which we might speak in cool detachment. When we understand mystery, we enter into it consciously and know it by sharing and by participation. Such understanding is not less intelligent than that which we achieve in objective knowledge; it is more intelligent. The essence of intellectual understanding is not the making of copies or mental replicas of things "out there." Understanding is not the fashioning of ideas; *it is conscious presence to the real, in whole or in part.* In the attempt to achieve real understanding of the mystery we will go to the limit of what can be thought and said, but we will not go beyond it. At that point, *but not before it,* we can pause and be silent, because silence at this point is also a word uttered by authentic faith.

There are many aspects to the mystery of the cross, but all of them are rooted in one fact: on the cross God took the brokenness of the world into himself; through the cross, God himself is in this lost and estranged world, making its abandonment and estrangement his own. The cross is the end of the way which began with Exodus 3:14 ("I will be there as the one that I will be"). God will be the one he wants to be, when and where he wants, on his own terms. His absolute freedom to be the one he wants to be is the miracle of a God whom we could never invent, a God we could not discover, a God who goes where he is not supposed to go, a God who dares to do what is in our eyes not fitting and proper. The real God will be here on his terms and not ours, and *for this reason* he will be the *one for us* and his power will be manifest in mercy. I believe that it will be useful to speak about this mystery under three different headings: God's *participation* in the human condition, God's *acceptance* of man without reserve, and God's *transformation* of man by this acceptance.

5.52 The man on the cross is the person whom the eternal God has sought as his counterpart forever. This Jesus is constituted as a human person by his dialogue with God. He is *within* the personal life of God and God is *within* the personal life of Jesus. Through Jesus, the broken being of the world enters the personal life of the everlasting God, and this God shares in the broken being of the world. God is eternally committed to this world, and this commitment becomes full and final in his personal presence within this weak and broken man on the cross. In him, the eternal one takes our destiny upon himself—a destiny of estrangement, separation, meaninglessness and despair. *But at this moment the emptiness and alienation that mar and mark the human situation become once and for all, in time and in eternity, the ways of God. God is with this broken man in suffering and in failure, in darkness and at the edge of despair, and for this reason suffering and failure, darkness and hopelessness will never again be signs of the separation of man from God.* God *identifies* himself with the man on the cross, and for this reason everything that we think of as manifesting the absence of God will, for the rest of time, be capable of manifesting his presence—up to and including death itself.

Jesus is rejected and his mission fails, but God participates in this failure, so that failure itself can become a vehicle of his presence, his being here for us. Jesus is weak, but this weakness is God's own, and so weakness itself can become something to glory in. Jesus' death exposes the weakness and insecurity of our situation, but God has made them his own; at the end of the road, where abandonment is total and all the props are gone, *he is there.* At the moment when an abyss yawns beneath the shaken foundations of the world and the self, God is there, in the depths, and the abyss becomes a ground. Because God was in this broken man who died on the cross, although our hold on existence is fragile, and although we walk in the shadow of death all the days of our lives, and although we live under the spell of a nameless dread against which we can do nothing, the message of the cross is good news indeed: rejoice in your fragility and weakness; rejoice even in that nameless dread, because God has been there and nothing can separate you from him. It has all been conquered, not by any power in the world or in yourself, but by God. When God takes death into himself, it means not the end of God but the end of death. This is the point of Paul's magnificent profession of faith in Romans 8:31–39. Paul knows that there is "nothing in heaven or on earth . . . not even life or death" which can separate him from the love of God that has become manifest in Jesus Christ. Paul draws up an impressive little litany of things that are commonly regarded as capable of separating man from God and then triumphantly announces that none of them have the power to do this, after all. There is such a thing as a false triumphalism that should have no place in the Church, but Paul's triumphant cry here is the center of the good news and it is a consequence of his theology of the cross. Nothing will ever be the same: sorrow is undercut by joy, despair by hope and death by life—and all this has come to pass because God himself is with this broken man who dies, stripped of all that had swayed the crowds and impressed even his own followers.

5.53 There is a second aspect to the mystery of the cross: it is the almost incredible paradox of God's judgment on man which is at the same time God's *unconditional acceptance* of man. In Jesus,

God becomes involved with the world in such a way that from now on the world is not simply God's creation but his destiny. The world's future becomes God's future and our history becomes forever his. In Jesus, God creates historical truth, and this historical truth which he creates is his act of unconditionally accepting, affirming, sustaining and supporting us. *To identify one's destiny with that of another, to make another's future my own, is the highest form of acceptance and the ultimate act of "wanting the other to be."* Such an acceptance is not a distant act of condescension. It is an act of love which is nothing less than all-encompassing forgiveness and all-inclusive claim. It is forgiveness because God will not allow anything to separate us from him. It is a total claim because one who completely shares the destiny of another has created a zone of intimacy so profound that this other may be claimed with the same immediacy and totality with which one lays claim to one's own talents, energy, and self.

God's acceptance of man is total, but in accepting us he lays claim to us with equal totality, and this claim is at the same time a *judgment* on us which affirms what is true and rejects what is false. The cross is a judgment on the all-too-human self of man on his own. The human animal is finite and weak, lonely and insecure, but we find this impossible to face, and we resist this with all of our energy, making ourselves into absolutes and resolutely denying that we are weak. We identify the partial truth we have reached with ultimate truth. We identify the limited goodness we have attained with absolute goodness. We attribute absoluteness to our own achievements and to those of our culture. In short, we try to achieve security by invading the sphere of the divine, by playing God.

But this attempt is doomed, and this is made manifest by the death of the individual, by the collapse of all-encompassing intellectual systems (Hegelianism and medieval Scholasticism would be good examples here), by the bankruptcy of those moral systems which offer man self-salvation through strength of will (Pharisaism and Puritanism would be good examples here), by the decay of every brilliant culture and the decline of every all-powerful empire.

The cross is a judgment against the self which is man's creation. God is there, in and with this broken man. In Jesus, the weakness of man and the doom of his temporal aspirations become the medium of his unconditional affirmation by God, and this marks the end of our delusions of grandeur, of our pretensions to have a claim on man and God because of our intelligence, our personal magnetism, or our moral goodness. We are always tempted to make of these and other good qualities *absolutes*, ultimates, worthy of any sacrifice, because through them we achieve an (illusory!) security of our own. As such they exercise a truly demonic and destructive role in our lives. But paradoxically, when they are "de-demonized" by the cross, stripped of their claim to absoluteness, they can be accepted and enjoyed. Freed *from* them as absolutes, we are freed *for* them; no longer there to serve our manipulative drives, we can make use of them to serve others. Again here the cross shows itself not as the source of a sad and morbid view of life, but rather as the ground of a free and joyous humanism.

The cross is God's judgment not in the sense of punishment inflicted but rather in the sense that it is God's assertion about what is false and what is true in us. Like all of God's judgments, it leads not to condemnation but to life. On the cross, all of the implications of creaturehood in a world under the power of sin are manifest. But if the truth of this is accepted, then God can be Creator again, and this is the deepest meaning of his judgment: the cross is the offer of a new life.

5.54 This brings us to the third aspect of the mystery of the cross. For Jesus, weakness, suffering, death at the edge of despair—all of these were ways of being with God, despite the evidence that God himself had gone. Because of what happened on the cross, *a new way of existing has become a reality in the world: faith.* The suffering and vulnerability of man which, up to that moment, had been indices of the absence of God and of man's separation from him can now become ways of expressing and realizing reliance on God and experiencing his nearness. The limitations and inadequacies which formerly embarrassed us can now become occasions of "boasting" (Paul's word), because, infinitely more than our merits, they give us a claim on God and he has shown that he will always honor this claim. There is a paradox here which undercuts all that is really problematic about human life: the apparently meaningless has meaning. Some good lines on this aspect of the cross were written by Hans Georg Koch in the *Herder-Korrespondenz* for March 1975:

> It is almost belaboring the obvious to point out that the cross is the sharpest protest against an understanding of man which wants to see him only as healthy, young, successful, etc., and therefore recommends that he do everything possible to avoid the encounter with suffering in every form. From the vantage point of the cross it would have to be said that when man suffers he has the task of "accepting wholly and entirely the situation which is bearing in upon him, integrating it and transforming it into an aspect of his own self-actualization, so that he decides for God in his suffering and so that the destructive situation itself becomes a positive aspect of his personal decision . . ." (citation from Rahner's *Theological Dictionary*). One can learn from suffering, and a banal optimism whose prescription for life is apathy leads to a loss of sensitivity for reality in general. But sensitivity for suffering, when it is based on Jesus, does not mean the glorification of suffering, which leads either to masochism or to an apathetic coming to terms with things simply because they are

there. Jesus was the man for others not simply in his sufferings on the cross, but also in all of the things he did to free men, to heal the sick, to put an end to oppressive law and to forgive guilt. Therefore, if the Christian's place is first of all with those who suffer, who are stripped of their rights, who are oppressed and who cannot help themselves, that does not mean that happiness is an object of suspicion.

5.55 This new way of existing which is empowered by the cross can be described as faith, but it could also be called *life in freedom*. In and through the cross of Jesus, God is here, liberating us from ourselves. The new "stance" which becomes possible as a result of this liberation could be spoken of in these terms: What God wants is the one thing necessary; we are at his disposal and not ours, and this is the root of our peace and our joy. Our "honor", position, reputation and the like become quite unimportant, and even a little silly. And yet, there is no pretense or pathos about giving them up, but rather a kind of wry humor that we or others could ever have taken them seriously. The insecurity of life is admitted quite frankly, along with our inability to do much about it. There is a sense of leaving the future up to God, as far as its ultimate meaning goes, but also there is the realization that this is justified only after we have done everything in our power to bring God's future about through our own careful thought, shrewd planning and hard work. There is a calm awareness that God is the source of everything, including our practical dedication to his tasks, and there is the realization that this God is *faithful*. There is an awareness of the gifts that God has given and a freedom to accept these happily and un-self-consciously, rejoicing in them precisely as gifts, realizing that they are given to us for the service of others, but realizing that we should enjoy using them for others and not make this into an ascetical burden. This comes down to accepting God's love with joy and handing it on in the same spirit. Such a person will show a strange combination of careful prudence and the willingness to take real risks, which will be incomprehensible to anyone who has not experienced the liberation which comes from the cross of Christ.[258]

The cross empowers faith, but we should remember that this is not exclusively a relation with God, but works *through* this relation to affect all. On the cross, one man "stands in" for us all. He it is who lets God be God and he it is to whom we owe the fact that we now are sons and daughters of this Father. In the man on the cross God has given us everything, and because Jesus Christ "stood in" for us, we have the joyous task of standing in for others, assuming responsibility for them and loving them. The cross does not tell us directly *how* to do this, but like the rest of the Christian message of which it is the heart and center it gives us the freedom to use our heads intelligently for others and not to misuse them in the service of our own selfish and manipulative drives. The cross relativizes all the norms of the world, all the accepted standards and conventions of society and even of a Church which is constantly tempted to become too comfortable in the world, and too confident in deciding where God is and how he is to be found.

The cross empowers faith and it makes life in freedom a possibility. The cross can do this because it not only judges man's attempt to play God; it also judges man's attempt to *define* God, to specify where God is and how he must be found, to determine where he may show himself and how it is appropriate for him to act. In this sense, the cross is a judgment against religion itself. Ideally, religion is man's search for God; in practice, it always contains strong elements of man's desire to "domesticate" God. Religious man attempts to "locate" God, ostensibly in the desire to go there and serve him. Religious man creates sacred realms and distinguishes them with care from the secular and the profane—sacred times and sacred places, sacred persons, sacred buildings and sacred seasons. But the barrier between the sacred and the profane, ostensibly raised for the glory of God, in reality confines God to a sacred preserve and leaves man lord in his own world. The cross is the symbol and the reality of God's presence in the world, of his refusal to be confined to the realm of the sacred, and of his act of laying claim to the secular and the profane. *The cross brings about the final desacralization of man's relationship with God.* The cross manifests the humanity of God, and it is a permanent critique of the inhumanity which lurks in much religious practice.

5.6 The Resurrection

This brings us almost to the end of a chapter that has tried to answer the question of why the cross is a saving event, and it might seem appropriate now, after a few concluding remarks, to turn to the resurrection. However, there will be no separate or additional chapter about the resurrection, for the simple reason that we have been speaking about the resurrection since the beginning of this chapter. If this statement seems strange or even preposterous, consider the following facts.

5.61 It is clear from the texts of Mark and Paul (the author of the first Gospel to be written and the author of the earliest material to be incorporated into the New Testament) that the cross is in no sense a sad or tragic interlude in the life of Jesus, through which he had to pass, but which was then to be reversed, nullified or expunged from the record by some subsequent event. Paul and Mark speak in different accents, but each is insistent that the cross is not to be forgotten. However, it is not only a question of remembering the cross; for both Mark and Paul it is not really a past event at all, in the sense that it could be confined to an interval of time in the recent or distant past. Mark quite evidently wrote his Gospel to keep the death of

the Lord in the forefront of the Christian mind and heart at a
time when it was threatened with being relegated to the past.
And for Paul, Jesus, the living Lord, remains the crucified one. A
careful reading of Mark and Paul leads inescapably to this conclusion: to proclaim that the cross is a saving event and to
proclaim that on the cross of Christ both God and man are
redefined is to affirm that God has raised Jesus from the dead—
that is, it is to affirm that *Jesus Christ lives,* and that this one who
lives is precisely Jesus who was crucified.

The meaning of the resurrection is this: that Jesus who had
died did not remain dead, but is now alive, really, personally,
physically. In some respects the picture of the resurrection that
we find in the New Testament is confusing. The stories of the
empty tomb and of the appearances of the Lord, which we find
in Matthew, Luke and John (the apparition account in Mark is
not part of the original Gospel), are difficult to reconcile with
each other; and yet one thing is perfectly clear: all of the men
who shared in writing the New Testament were convinced that
Jesus had really died but had not remained dead. They knew
that God had called him from the land of the dead to the land of
the living. If we read between the lines of their stories, it
becomes clear that when Jesus died, his followers were in no way
predisposed for his resurrection or even ready to believe in it. It
was only hesitantly and, one might say, unwillingly that they
began to accept the fact that their crucified teacher and friend
was now alive and was their Lord. (And it was probably their
growing awareness that he had returned, not to the ordinary
human life which they all were living, but to a more complete,
authentic and real life, that made them describe him and his
appearances in a way which makes it extremely difficult to derive
from their accounts a series of events accurately ordered in
space and time.) The New Testament authors are really not
interested in "proving" the resurrection, but it is this very fact

which makes their witness to the resurrection more valuable and more convincing. We might say that the New Testament itself as an *existing fact* is the real evidence for the resurrection. This is an extremely important point and it needs some clarification, which the Gospel of Mark can provide.

As is clear from the earlier sections of this chapter, Mark gives us a very profiled theology of the cross. But Mark gives us no accounts of the appearances of Jesus to his followers after his death (as noted above, the Markan text after 16:9 is a later addition). For Mark it is evident that Jesus lives *now*—that is, in Mark's own community in Mark's own day. For Mark, it is unnecessary to speak of Jesus' appearances years ago, because Jesus is with them *now* in the preaching of the community and in the Eucharist which the community celebrates. The important thing is to find out who this Jesus *is*—that is, the same one who in life and in death redefined the relationship of man and God who continues to do this today for all those who are willing to accept the critical power of the cross in their lives.

What this means is that wherever and whenever the word of the cross is really a word of power—that is, whenever and wherever the word of the cross transforms both the individual and the community—then this word of the cross *itself* is convincing evidence that Jesus lives. Why? Because a living Lord is the only possible ground and basis of such a word! If Jesus had died and remained dead, his death might have been sad or even tragic, but it would not have been significant. If Jesus had died and remained good and dead, then his definitions of both God and man would have been unmasked as instances of hopelessly wishful thinking (and this is what Paul means when he affirms that both preaching and faith are without content unless Jesus rose from the dead). In this respect Jesus differs radically from Socrates and from any and all of the more or less mythical heroes and noble figures whose deaths are presented as shining examples of honor and integrity. Unless Jesus lives, the word of the cross is sheer stupidity; but the converse is also true: if the word of the cross is worth preaching, and if, when preached, it really empowers life in freedom, then this fact itself is irrefutable evidence that the resurrection took place. A theology of the cross which shows that the cross was not the tragic end of one man but the definitive saving intervention of God in history *is* a theology of the resurrection in the only sense in which such a theology can be a Christian endeavor at all.

5.62 For more than a century the discussion about the resurrection has been carried on in a way which makes it somewhat difficult to see the point being made here. Quite often no attempt was made to define terms accurately, and even more often there was a single-minded concentration on secondary issues. In fact, discussion was often pre-empted by defensive and misguided apologetics which, in turn, rested on poor exegesis. We have to be clear about one very important fact: the reality of the resurrection and the firmness of our faith in it do not rest on fundamentalist "exegesis." On the contrary, faith is very poorly served by such a parody of reverence for the word of God. These remarks are, of course, double-edged. On the one hand, they are critical of those who insist on finding more in the apparition narratives of the New Testament than is really being affirmed there, and who want to impose a particular model of resuscitation in the name of Christian faith. But these remarks are, on the other hand, equally critical of those who reduce the resurrection to a kind of vague "being with God" and who are careless of the full individual, personal, conscious *humanity* of the risen Lord. There is much about the nature of the resurrection and about the form of the risen body which is debatable. But if the word *body* means "that in virtue of which we are personally present to one another in conscious dialogue, in space and in time," then the *bodily* resurrection of Jesus (in *this*

sense) is not a mere interpretation, but is of the very substance
of our faith.

The whole question needs to be rethought today, and here,
as elsewhere, it will become apparent that a truly critical exegesis does not destroy faith but strengthens it, and, in fact, provides for the term "bodily resurrection of Jesus" a content
which is indispensable for faith. Without going into the exegesis
of the resurrection narratives themselves, I believe that it will be
useful here to present a series of thesis-like statements about the
resurrection, which will suggest the direction that our thought
on this central mystery of our faith should take, and will do this
by defining the resurrection itself in terms of the cross and in
terms of the truth which became historical and permanent on
that cross.

5.7 Ten Theses on the Resurrection

1. The word *resurrection* has two distinct meanings. On the
one hand it is used to refer to an *act,* and on the other it is used
to refer to the lasting result of that act.

2. The resurrection as act is the immediate intervention of
God in history. The resurrection as the lasting result of that act
is the fact that Jesus who died now lives. Even more simply, the
resurrection as lasting result is *the living Jesus.* This, the fact that
Jesus lives, is the content of our faith in the resurrection. Speculation about how the resurrection took place and what else it
might involve should be carefully distinguished from faith. It is
not a sign of faith to force the resurrection to conform to our
ideas of what the resuscitation of a dead man might be like, and
it is not a sign of faith to identify bodily resurrection with such a
model.

3. The resurrection as act does not reverse or nullify the
cross, nor does it relativize what was definitively achieved on the
cross. Rather, it makes the cross and the definition of God and

man which was realized there *permanently valid.* The resurrection, therefore, as the lasting result of God's act, is the permanent presence of Jesus, who is and *remains* the crucified Lord.

4. This Jesus who lives is not simply the one who was (among other things) crucified. He *is* essentially the crucified one and it is as such that he calls us to discipleship.

5. Jesus did not return to an ordinary earthly life, but the life which he now has (and which coincides with the resurrection as lasting effect) is a personal existence, distinct from that of *God(nt).* To affirm that Jesus lives is to affirm that he is a person in dialogue with *God(nt),* and in communion with us, and therefore touching the world of space and time as a conscious participant in dialogue, although not entirely encompassed by that world. In this sense, to affirm that Jesus lives is to affirm his *bodily resurrection.*

6. The resurrection as a lasting result of God's act, that is, the resurrection as the fact that Jesus lives, is closely connected with the fact that the message of Jesus continues to be preached, but it is not to be identified with this fact. It is the apparent futility and "ignobility" of Jesus' death which makes this identification impossible. Jesus' death was, to all appearances, meaningless and wasteful. He did not die as a martyr to any evident cause. Jesus' word about God and man was not self-validating. *God* validated it by raising Jesus from the dead. It is *because he lives* that his message can still be preached as true and transforming. It is vital here not to confuse cause and effect.

7. The resurrection, therefore, as a lasting result (that is, the fact that Jesus now lives) is the only possible cause, ground and basis for a kerygma or preaching about Jesus which is truly a word of power.

8. Therefore, the preaching of the cross, if it is truly a transforming word of power, is certain evidence for the fact that Jesus lives.

9. This preaching of the cross and this preaching of the

resurrection as the lasting result of God's action are inseparable. The first implies the second as inevitably as an effect implies its cause.

10. The New Testament has two very different approaches to the resurrection. The first approach is to recount stories of the appearances of the Lord to his followers, individually or in groups; the second approach is to record statements of the convictions of some early Christians (that is, the writers of the New Testament documents), that Jesus who had died now lives.

a. The stories of how Jesus appeared cannot be reduced to a series of secular events—that is, events which would be observable and recordable apart from faith. (It would be very odd if they could be!) There is a certain ambiguity about these appearance stories—an ambiguity which points to something unworldly or other-worldly about them. This ambiguity evidently did not bother the early Church, and there are few signs in the Gospels of attempts to remove it by harmonizing the apparition stories. These stories themselves can hardly be called a late development. Paul enumerates several in 1 Corinthians 15 as part of the official teaching which he himself had received after his conversion experience. Since it is difficult to give a date after 33 or 34 A.D. for Paul's conversion, and since the statement of the resurrection faith as he gives it already seems rather formal and stylized (which points to the fact that it already had its own history behind it), Paul's account brings us back quite near to the original events.

b. On the other hand, there is no ambiguity in the statements given by various New Testament writers of their conviction that Jesus who died now lives. They not only know that Jesus lives, but they affirm it in a way which would be inexplicable unless they were convinced that he was alive.

c. These statements of conviction are rooted in the certitude that the Lord had really appeared to his followers, individually and in groups, and was *really present* in the early Christian

communities. For Paul, the appearance of the Lord to the other
apostles is confirmed and verified by his appearance to him
(Paul). For Mark, the conviction that the Lord is present in
preaching and the Eucharist is so overwhelming that no apparition stories need be recounted.

d. Paul and Mark make it clear that it is the crucified Lord
who lives. I believe that it is in their proclamation of the transforming effect of the cross on individual and community that we
have the most genuinely Christian evidence for the resurrection.
This is the precise sense in which the cross and the resurrection
may be said to belong together or may be said to be two sides of
one and the same event.

5.8   A Final Word on the Cross

The word of the cross remains the power of God, and this is
the guarantee of the presence of the risen Lord among us. The
historical event belongs to the past, but as long as the cross is
understood and proclaimed, the death of the Lord is life-giving,
because it proclaims the paradoxical truth about the human
situation: no human life can effectively overcome finitude, sin
and tragedy, but God was in Christ who was crushed because he
had to bear the insupportable burden of all three. The cross
affirms that man is finite but it also affirms that God is with him
in his finitude. The cross makes evident the fact that man is
weak, but it tells him to glory in that weakness because God has
chosen to share this weakness. The cross exposes man's insecurity but it also tells him that God has made that insecurity his
own. The cross manifests the darkness in which man lives and
dies but it also tells him that when the darkness is most impene-
trable, God is there. The cross is the message that God is with us
in finitude, weakness, insecurity and darkness and that it is
precisely there that he affirms us with a love from which nothing
can separate us.

The faith which rests on the cross is not a faith of easy moral and intellectual certitudes, of untroubled security and of hope which is founded on accurate scenarios of the life hereafter. The cross offers certitude only at the moment at which the certitudes of this world crumble. The cross offers security when the foundations of human security are destroyed. The cross offers both this certitude and this security in the midst of a very great darkness because it affirms that the central moment of history occurred when God was driven out of the world onto a cross. The cross does not affirm that life is without meaning or that our free and responsible actions are without significance for eternal life. But the cross does assert that it is only in the power of the absolute "no" to all human pretensions of absoluteness, to all of our attempts to attribute ultimacy to ourselves and the work of our hands, that God's absolute "yes" will triumph and assure us of the eternity for which we yearn.

The message of the cross is a unique word to each of us who is willing to hear it, because it speaks to us where no one else has been and where we are now and where God chooses to be. In the man on the cross he came to stay, and until the end of time there will be no dark corner of human existence which will ever again be deprived of his presence. To hear and accept the word of the cross is to live in joy and to die in peace, secure in the knowledge that when the foundations shake, God is there, and will prove himself, as always, by "calling into being the things that are not and raising the dead to life."

Notes

1. This question will be discussed at greater length in the fourth chapter. The subtlety of the "religious" mind would be admirable if not so perverse. This is a good example of manipulating Jesus under the guise of showing him reverence.
2. The real theological question is never "Does God exist?" but rather "What kind of a God exists?" The "other gods" referred to here do not exist, of course, outside of the mind, but precisely as projections of the mind they possess great destructive power.
3. In other words, they *found out*, they discovered something they had not known before. No one other than God is at stake in Jesus' words and actions. This is the point which Mark makes quite clearly in 1:2–4, where the preparatory work of John the Baptist is interpreted by means of the text from Second Isaiah. The *Lord* (Yahweh) is coming.
4. The idioms are different, but the thought is remarkably constant. Some examples: John 14:6 ("I am the way, the truth and the life. No one comes to the Father but through me"). In Mark 1:27 and 2:12, Jesus is the one who teaches with "authority"—that is, he brings the creative, originating power of God himself to bear on a situation. He does not merely comment on something that God did, and in this he is very different from the teachers of the law. For Paul, in Romans 1:16–17, the good news (which Paul can, on other occasions, identify with Jesus Christ) is simply "the power of God." In Colossians 1:15, Christ is the "image of the unseen God." Finally, in Hebrews 1:2, God is *definitively* present in his Son—this is the meaning of the phrase "in these last days."
5. Faith does not provide new principles on the basis of which we proceed to make moral judgments. Faith liberates us to use our heads, and it is in *willing* to act *intelligently* that we act rightly and well.
6. This does not mean that theology adds to the *content* of faith (in

198

the sense that theological propositions would belong to the object of faith). What I want to underline is the fact that the act of faith demands thought and reflection, as a condition of being true to itself.

7. No one else can either. Words are symptoms of the health of the society that uses them, and speech which is empty and devoid of meaning is a sign of a society which is without purpose. A society which cultivates jargon is devoting its energies to creating a wall between itself and reality.

8. This definition of theology does not imply that God can be known in the same way in which we know things. God is not an object and there can be no purely objective knowledge of God.

9. This silence will be fruitful and productive only when we have gone to the very limits of what words can affirm.

10. A so-called "negative" theology is not the denial of the knowledge of God nor is it the renunciation of the attempt to speak about God. It is real knowledge and it is constituted by awareness of the distance which separates God himself from every word about him.

11. Knowledge of God is never a purely theoretical matter. (Real knowledge never is, under any circumstances.) It is for this reason that faith (which is always *knowledge*) has the power to save.

12. Because the question of God (*theos*) is always the question of Jesus. All theology is Christology.

13. The New Testament passages in which the title appears are almost certainly constructions of the community and products of the Easter faith. When the title *was* applied to Jesus, it was an excellent way of affirming the Church's faith in the risen Lord, who had given the term new meaning by his cross. For this reason, it is even more certain that Jesus did not use or seek the title. Before his death it was not "serviceable."

14. According to Mark 8:31–38 Jesus will accept the title only on his own terms—that is, when he redefines it in terms of suffering.

15. This is not to deny that faith comes from hearing, but it underlines the fact that it is not a hearing of statements *about* God, but rather that God himself is present in the word that is heard.

16. The word "see" in this connection refers to an experience which is direct and not mediated. This is why Paul emphasizes his encounter with Jesus on the road to Damascus, but it is *also* his reason for referring to preaching as "the power of God." Faith

can and must come through hearing because the risen Lord *himself* is present in the preached word.

17. This universal meaning of Jesus as the Christ is one that never leaves the unique historical event behind. Of all the ways of dividing Jesus Christ, this is the most dangerous and the most common. This is why the search for the historical Jesus (not necessarily in the form it took in the nineteenth century) is a permanent part of Christology.

18. We are social animals not really because we need things, information or support from each other. We are social because we depend on each other not only for our physical existence, but for our personal being, our selfhood.

19. This is the basis of the moral demand of truthfulness. We are, quite literally, as good as our word.

20. Words, therefore, transcend some of the limits of space and time. *Some* words transcend all such limits, and these are the words which are, in the proper sense of the word, revelatory.

21. Obviously, I can keep watch over the mediation of my word only if I am alive. Only then can others find *me* in this word, and not merely the memory of what I have been and done.

22. People resented the fact that he had not been "commissioned." The contemptuous reference to "the carpenter" in Mark 3 probably preserves the memory of this attitude. Jesus never pointed to his qualifications; he always acted as though what he said and did was transparent to the one who sent him.

23. Since the Reformation the opposition of Word and Sacrament has been fateful for the Catholic-Protestant confrontation. An understanding of the fact that words are needed to interpret actions (and that the word is the decisive element of the action) and that the non-verbal elements of action give concreteness and definition to words has a great contribution to make to intelligent dialogue among Christians.

24. The New Testament practice, rather strange to us, of "creating" words of the Lord in order to solve new problems which the Church faced in the later first century is an indication of this. The Lord is not really the one remembered; he is the one who lives.

25. See the end of the last chapter for a more complete discussion of the resurrection.

26. It is important to emphasize again that faith is not a form of knowing which can dispense with experience. Faith is grounded in

experience, although it is an experience of a different kind.

27. Genuine existence is not *a* "given," to be identified with the brute fact of "being there." Genuine existence is *human* existence, and it is given in the sense that we receive it from others and cannot fashion it ourselves.

28. This is what characterizes Jesus' word. His hearers could not distance themselves from it or objectify it. Typically, his parables have the structure of Nathan's parable to David in 2 Samuel 12:1–14 ("You are the man . . .").

29. In Paul this theme is strong. It is precisely in having this new *Lord* and in belonging to this sphere of influence that we are free of the "powers"—the iron laws of fate which govern human life.

30. Quite the opposite, as is clear from 1 Corinthians 1 and 2.

31. This is the real meaning of Paul's doctrine of justification. It is not something that God *does* (among many other things), but it is what God *is*. For Paul the cross is central because it is there that God "justifies" the sinner, accepts the unacceptable.

32. There is a striking example of this in the antitheses of the Sermon on the Mount (Mt 5:21–48). Jesus relativizes the law of Moses in a way which is not reconcilable with the typically Jewish-Christian logion of Matthew 5:17 ("Whoever sets aside even the most insignificant prescription of the law . . ."). The same tendencies can be seen in Mark 2:18–20, where the bold (and almost mocking) word about fasting and its inappropriateness, now that Jesus is here, is tempered by a community which was eager to reintroduce the practice of fasting, which it then justified with the incredible assertion that when the community is left without the visible presence of the earthly Jesus, everything will revert to the *status quo ante*.

33. But it is, like all of God's judgments, a rejection of what is false in man and therefore an *affirmation* of man. This theme will be developed in Chapter 5.

34. This is the key to understanding Mark's Gospel. Mark does not write to preserve the memory of a great and noble man (much less a demigod); he writes so that the community will not forget that the risen Lord, who lives in their midst, is the one who defined himself through suffering and dying.

35. That is, the New Testament word is not precisely the word *about* Jesus. It is rather *his own word*, as mediated in the event of its reception by his followers.

202   *Notes*

36. As will be evident, this does not mean that the most important task of exegesis is to determine which events "really happened" and which did not. This would be a parody of historical-critical method. The facile distinction between what "really happened" and what did not is an almost certain guarantee that the text of the New Testament will not be understood and that the essentially symbolic nature of *all* language has not been grasped.

37. Not that we have to know the history and etymology of the words we already know in order to speak and understand. But we do have to know the meaning of all the words we use, and for "new" words—that is, those which come from alien historical and cultural contexts—this is possible only if the words can be located within these contexts.

38. *Kerygma* is precisely the word which transcends the limitations of time while remaining historical.

39. Not in the general sense in which proclamation intends the *conversion* of those who hear it, but rather what the proclamation *means to assert*. Word meanings are often not obvious, and respect for this fact demands that word meanings be approached critically. If a word is or claims to be the word of God, the need for critical method to find its meaning is even greater.

40. This is an important distinction. Much of what was "believed" in the so-called "ages of faith" was and is a scandal to Christian faith. It is not a good thing to believe as many things as possible. It is a bad thing to demand of oneself or others in the name of faith what Jesus of Nazareth did not demand.

41. I would prefer to use the word *intelligence* here, but the antithesis is usually expressed in terms of faith and *reason*. This represents an unfortunate narrowing of the discussion and tends to obscure the fact that the use of practical and theoretical reason, in natural science and other areas, rests on a commitment and decision which has a structure very similar to that of the act of faith.

42. This *made-for-faith* structure of reason was developed at some length by Paul Tillich in Volume One of his *Systematic Theology*. See also Chapters 2 and 4 of my doctoral dissertation, *Paul Tillich's Theology of the Cross* (Tübingen, 1973).

43. To a remarkable degree, the New Testament writers disappear behind their writings. Some deductions can be made about them, but they do not assume the profiled stance of biographers. The Gospels are, in every sense of the word, community writings.

44. Except for Paul, either the New Testament writers are unknown, or the writings are attributed to persons who, in fact, did not write them. Attempts to deny this are almost always based on apologetic motives—that is, convictions of what must be true if the New Testament is to be used in a certain way.
45. That is, that the New Testament be *proclamation* and not historiography.
46. This theme is superbly developed in Willi Marxsen's *The New Testament as the Church's Book* (Fortress, 1972).
47. There is much ambiguity in the "historical Jesus." Even the rather superficial sense defended by Biehl ("Jesus insofar as he can be made the object of critical-historical research") gives us a Jesus who would support this affirmation. Cf. P. Biehl, *Theologische Revue*, 1956/7, 55: "Zur Frage nach dem historischen Jesus."
48. The messianic secret is Mark's way of safeguarding the humanity of Jesus. Its purpose was not apologetic and defensive, as Wrede argued.
49. Note that it is only in Matthew and Luke that the theophany is public. According to Mark, Jesus alone hears the Father's word of approval.
50. Strangely enough, the strongest texts in support of these contrasting views seem to belong to the pre-Pauline tradition. This is true of both Philippians 2:5–11 and, probably, of Romans 1:4.
51. As will be seen in the third chapter, this is not precisely what was asserted by the christological and trinitarian councils, but it seems safe to say that it was tacitly accepted by the overwhelming majority of council fathers.
52. The role played by the historical Jesus, not in motivating faith but in specifying its content, is identical to the role played by the cross in 1 Corinthians 1 and 2, from which these words come.
53. The "competitive" view of the divine and human in Jesus is the most destructive legacy of this lengthy process of de-emphasizing the humanity of Jesus. This process began before the New Testament was completed, but it became dominant only in the Greek patristic period.
54. Over the years, the canons and norms of interpretation have changed, and this century has seen the acceptance, both *de jure* and *de facto,* in Catholic theology, of a critical approach to the biblical text which was, in practice, categorically rejected by the Pontifical Biblical Commission in its *Responsa* of the first decade of

this century. This whole question remains the most serious unresolved problem of Catholic ecclesiology.

55. *Humani Generis*, NCWC Edition, Washington, D.C., 1951, paragraph 21, lines 2 to 5. Note also the reference at the end of the first paragraph to the encyclical *Inter Gravissimas* of Pius IX, October 28, 1870.

56. Etymologically the term is an excellent description of exactly what happened. In practice, however, it came to mean that "Jesus'" message about the fatherhood of God and the brotherhood of man was lost. Whatever such vague terms might mean, they miss the point of Jesus' message, and the term "Hellenization of the Gospel" has associations with liberal theology which make it unusable today.

57. Catholic theology finally took note of this at Vatican II; see the *Constitution on Divine Revelation*, chapter 2, n. 10.

58. In the Johannine tradition, the role of the Spirit is to make clear the meaning of all that Jesus said and did.

59. Catholic theological traditionalists are not very comfortable with this fact and often deal with it by arguing that the words used by the councils are true "in the sense intended by the Church." This solution is formally correct, but it reduces conciliar statements to the level of a monologue of the management sector of the Church with itself. The councils deserve better than this.

60. I believe that it is beyond question that the *intention* of all of the councils was to remain true to Scripture. The degree to which this was achieved was another question.

61. This could only have been achieved if these same philosophies could have been used in a self-critical way. But they could not and this is the root problem of the whole conciliar period.

62. For the first two decades of its existence, the Church was almost exclusively a Jewish sect. Practically speaking, one had to be a Jew in order to be a Christian.

63. Not nearly enough importance is attributed to the fact that half of the New Testament was written by a man whose conversion came after the death, resurrection and ascension of Jesus. Reflection on this fact will lead to a far more nuanced view of what it means to say that Jesus founded the Church.

64. That is, the Church ceased to be *Palestinian* Jewish. Diaspora Judaism had strong universalist tendencies and in other respects too it was more capable of assimilating specifically Christian

teaching than Palestinian Judaism was. Both the early post-apostolic writing called *The Shepherd of Hermas* and the somewhat later *Second Letter of Clement* are productions of diaspora Judaism and they are good examples of the great difference between it and the traditionalist faith of the homeland.

65. This is the essential element of messianism: God *will* intervene definitively. The italicized word is so important that it is possible to separate messianism from Messiah, and on a later day it will even be possible to secularize the notion entirely (as Marxism has done).

66. They spoke the same language, in the ordinary sense of the word, but they had different resources of thought and expression at their disposal and therefore they did not speak the same language in the broad sense of the word.

67. This was the occasion of Paul's own development of the theology of the cross in 1 Corinthians 1 and 2.

68. The Third Council of Constantinople in the year 687 marks the traditional end of the patristic period, but the great battles were really over by 451. After the Council of Chalcedon, rear-guard actions were being fought, but by and large theology was subordinated to politics and was used as an instrument of imperial policy.

69. Most notably in Isaiah 40:12–31; this magnificent passage is remarkable for its bold statement of the total concern for man of the absolutely transcendent God.

70. In the so-called "myth of the cave"—Plato's allegory of human knowledge—those in the cave are imprisoned: bound with chains and unable to move their heads.

71. The strange doctrine of individuation by prime matter is both source and symptom of this inability to deal with the unique person. The ultimate ground of individuality is non-being!

72. According to this philosophy, God and man are free precisely in respect to *limited* goods and values. Therefore God cannot freely love himself.

73. Only a divinized humanity could fulfill such a role for the Greek mind and hence the attraction of those theories in which, in fact if not in so many words, the humanity of Jesus is absorbed into the divinity.

74. This also coexisted with strong statements of the power to "see" God, as in Exodus 24:11.

75. Paul's confrontation with the resurrection theology of the Corin-

thian "Christians" was the archetypal meeting of Christianity with the Greek mind.

76. Strangely enough, we find the most "advanced" Christology in the New Testament both in the first New Testament writer—Paul—and in the last of the Gospels to be written—that of John.

77. This problem of the historical Jesus goes far beyond the determination of what can be known of Jesus by the application of critical method to the sources. Too often, this remains an attempt to find at least a minimum of biographical material. The "New Quest," in the hands of Käsemann, Bornkamm, Schweizer and others, identifies the real Jesus with the impact of his word and work—with that in him which both justified the proclamation about him and was prolonged in that very proclamation.

78. The interest of the community was not biographical or historical. It was *kerygmatic.* What was at stake was the proclamation and the grounding of that proclamation in something that really happened.

79. The few texts which seem to do this are questionable on textual grounds.

80. There is no suggestion in the Prologue of John's Gospel that the Logos who is in some way "with" God then encounters a distinct human subjectivity in Jesus.

81. The resistance of Isaiah and Jeremiah to their prophetic vocations are the most notable examples of this.

82. John usually does this with the absolute "the Son," while for Paul the preferred term is "his Son."

83. I believe that John's Gospel could be called the last major writing of the New Testament. The pastoral and "catholic" epistles were written after this time, and 2 Peter may well have been written after the year 130.

84. Again, Palestinian Judaism did this, but see note 64.

85. This peculiar position is really a consequence of Aristotle's conception of knowledge as essentially *passive:* the thing known *changes* the knower, and therefore an immutable God could not possibly know the world.

86. This is the role played by the "God" of the elite in Book XII of Plato's *Laws.*

87. This is the real meaning of "emanation" and therefore it is not as rigidly and ineluctably pantheistic as it would seem to be.

88. That is, the intermediary—it is this intermediary which is usually identified with the Creator.

89. This is the Johannine term which underlines the distinction of Jesus from God and gives to such phrases as "The Father and I are one" their almost unbearable tension.

90. Philo (born about 30 B.C. and died about 45 A.D.) is the best known example, but evidence of the influence of Greek thought from the third century B.C. on is growing.

91. This category emphasized both unity and distinction.

92. An indication of this is that even among the apostolic Fathers the word *theos* might be used in the predicate when talking of Jesus, but the nominative *ho theos* was reserved for the Father.

93. See especially Ignatius' *Epistle to the Ephesians,* 7:2, where he calls Christ "gennetos kai agennetos . . . en sarki genomenos theos" (generated and ingenerate, God born in the flesh).

94. Although some of the terms (specifically *gennetos* kai *agennetos*) almost certainly did not have the technical meaning they were later to acquire.

95. It is interesting to note that Ignatius' city of Antioch was the only place where non-allegorical exegesis of Scripture was held in high repute during the whole patristic period.

96. However, the Apologists were not really speculating on God's being in itself, but precisely as knowable by us.

97. That is, they depersonalized the notion and made it a *qualitative* description.

98. This was above all true because of Clement's doctrine of the perfect *apatheia* of Jesus—that is, his immunity to any real change in or threat to his existence. Since emotions and other *pathe* are rooted in the soul, it is difficult to think of how Clement could have accepted the existence of a soul in Jesus.

99. This happened precisely to the degree to which the Logos assumed "personal" characteristics in the modern sense of the word.

100. That is, the ambiguity of the "second" divine being, who was, of course, needed to insure the isolation of the remote God from the world.

101. Constantine apparently took the last word of his legendary vision seriously and literally ("In hoc signo vinces").

102. The word *translation* is very important here and even more impor-

tant in the discussion about Chalcedon. It should never be assumed that the words which have traditionally been used to
translate the technical vocabulary of the early councils are really
adequate or accurate.

103. See Karl Rahner's essay in Volume One of *Theological Investigations,*
"God in the New Testament."

104. This was the perduring problem which Greek theology would face
in trying to come to terms with the cross. Generally, it saw the
cross as some kind of verification or proof of the reality of the
incarnation but was unable to attribute to the cross any proper
role in salvation.

105. J. N. D. Kelly, *Early Christian Doctrines* (Harper and Row), is a
fascinating work to read in this connection. Grillmeier's *Christ in
Christian Tradition* (John Knox) is more detailed but less critical on
the question of terminology.

106. See Isaiah 40:12–31 again for a beautiful statement of the paradox
which this implies.

107. See Kelly, *op. cit.,* 265–266.

108. See his *De Trinitate* 5, 10 and 7, 7–9.

109. And this *may* have meant to Eusebius nothing more than his own
objective reality.

110. The obsession with the "divinity of Christ" on the part of Christians with a traditionalist bent is another symptom of the same
problem. The question of whether Jesus "is" God is really irrelevant until we know *what kind of God it is* that Jesus makes known.

111. This is true since the soul is the determining element of the
human composite and the subject of thought and emotion.

112. Epistle 101, 7.

113. Grillmeier, *Christ in Christian Tradition,* 315.

114. See Kelly, *op. cit.,* 306.

115. See Grillmeier, *op. cit.,* "The Language and Thought of Nestorius
at Ephesus," 451–463.

116. Nestorians always seem to have meant by the word "concrete
reality" but were understood (by Alexandrines) to mean "person
as subject of thought and action." The word "person" was ambiguous then as it is now.

117. See Grillmeier, *op. cit.,* 523–526.

118. I believe that it would be correct to see in the fashioning of such
linguistic conventions the proper role of the magisterium, at least
insofar as the latter is (quite properly) apologetic and defensive.

However, it also indicates the precise reason for which the councils cannot be treated as sources of theology in the same sense as Scripture.

119. The truth of the conciliar statements should not be assumed on the basis of a pre-conceived notion of the role of the magisterium in the Church. Such an approach is dishonest and needlessly timid. On the other hand, it can be cogently argued that the positions which denied the conciliar doctrine during the period in question run counter to the scriptural doctrine itself.

120. He did this most characteristically in his redefinition of the word "God" in terms of mercy, and it was precisely this new definition of his which aroused the most passionate opposition. Jesus was not crucified because he claimed to be the Messiah; he was crucified because he claimed to bring the good news of a God who welcomes the sinner into his company.

121. But like many others who recognized this fact, they assumed that they knew who "God" was and that the mystery of Jesus was that of his identity with *this* "God" that they knew.

122. It was the consubstantiality of the Spirit which was stated at First Constantinople (a council which also forcefully reaffirmed Nicaea).

123. This is from the dogmatic definition of Chalcedon. See Grillmeier, *op. cit.,* 544.

124. This is from Leo's Letter to Flavian. See Denzinger, *Enchiridion Symbolorum,* 29th ed., n. 144.

125. These obsolescent and idiomatic usages are not unconnected with the ordinary use of the word *person* (e.g. "search of the 'person,'" where the word really means "body"), but I believe that the word here is commonly felt to be used in so different a sense as to be, practically, a different word.

126. The "exceptions" are the very texts which are often used to prove the divinity of Jesus—that is, John 1:1, Romans 9:5, etc.

127. Again, the important texts here are not the obvious ones ("The Father and I are one") but references like Mark 1:2 where it is asserted that when Jesus comes, no one less than the *Kyrios,* that is, Yahweh himself, is implicated in his arrival.

128. In Justin Martyr, the more common form is still that the Logos was "in" Christ, but by the end of the century it was more usual to say that the Logos *was* Christ; see Grillmeier, *op. cit.,* 90.

129. This is an important point. The question of the divinity of "Jesus"

or of "Jesus Christ" is quite modern. For the ancient councils it was the divinity of the Logos which was the direct and immediate concern (even though, logically, this could be extended to Jesus Christ through the *communicatio idiomatum*).

130. In fact, what was now "included" within God was precisely the speaking and the hearing, the *dialogue*, which characterize distinct human persons.

131. The clearest statement is found in the first anathema of the Lateran Council of 649, where it is asserted that in God there is the same "divinity, nature, substance, supreme power, sovereign dominion, will, and uncreated operation": Denzinger, *op. cit.*, n. 254.

132. I believe that this is a fair statement of what was intended (at least by Leo) at Chalcedon. At the same time, it underlines the essentially *static* character of the definition.

133. See Denzinger, *op. cit.*, n. 144. In the Latin-speaking areas it was always easy for a more popular (and in some respects quite modern) notion of *person* to gain ground against the highly technical concept of *hypostasis*. Trinitarian speculation in theology has not been sufficiently critical of this development.

134. This is a common failing in those given to recreating past golden ages. Such golden ages are romantic reconstructions and the attempts to recreate them usually run counter to the inspiration of those who originally created something of value.

135. *Aeterni Patris*, in the year 1879.

136. See note 55.

137. On the more popular level Kee, Young, Froelich, *Understanding the New Testament,* is very good, as is Spivey, Smith, *The Anatomy of the New Testament.* On the level of exegesis of the Gospel text, Eduard Schweizer's *Good News According to Matthew* and his *Good News According to Mark* will not be surpassed for a long time. Raymond Brown's *The Gospel According to John* is in its own class: it summarizes modern critical exegesis, it breaks new ground in the understanding of this most mysterious of Gospels, and it is at once critical and devotional.

138. This is a good and practical definition of exegesis: to say in our words today what the biblical writers said in their words then.

139. I use the term here not to refer to Jesus as the object of biographical interest but rather as the object of "kerygmatic" interest—that is, to Jesus as one who defined himself and God in and through

the word that he preached, and whose word is, in its fundamental meaning, accessible to those willing to engage themselves in a critical and historical reading of the New Testament.

140. Albert Schweitzer, *Geschichte der Leben-Jesu-Forschung*, 6th ed. (Munich, 1966), 626. The later German editions contain some material never incorporated into the English translations.

141. Some of the most outstanding works in this connection were written by Bultmann's former students and associates—for example, Bornkamm's *Jesus of Nazareth*, Schweizer's *Jesus*, and Conzelmann's *Jesus*. Schillebeeckx' *Jesus: An Experiment in Christology* draws on much of this excellent material and adds an important treatment of the criteria for historical authenticity.

142. This is the case because Jesus' mystery consists in the fact that *precisely in his humanity* he transcends limits and definitions.

143. The third and fourth chapters of Mark's Gospel contain a number of pericopes which illustrate this.

144. It is likely that Luke's text of the first Beatitude ("poor") is closer to the original than is Matthew's ("poor in spirit").

145. This is not to say that a sound moral theology cannot be based on the New Testament; it is simply to note that Jesus did not enunciate general principles or moral norms which can be applied to individual cases.

146. This is very striking in Mark 2:13–17 and in the story of the healing of the paralytic in Mark 2:1–12.

147. This is the meaning of the "good news . . . of the rule of God" in Mark 1:14–15. The first seven chapters of Mark's Gospel are an illustration of what this "rule" is which has come in Jesus.

148. See Schweizer, *Neotestamentica* 51–149.

149. It is often enough argued that Jesus identified himself with the messianic figure of the suffering servant of Second Isaiah, but this argument is worthless for two reasons: the *Jesus* material of the New Testament contains no clear references to the suffering servant, and in Second Isaiah the servant is *not* a messianic figure (Cyrus the Persian is!).

150. Mk 1:27. The juxtaposition of authority with his *new* (here in the sense of "definitive," "final") teaching is characteristic.

151. The Greek here is not *nea* (new as distinct from old) but *kaine* (radically new, in the sense that it will never grow old).

152. The Marcan texts in question cannot be interpreted merely as the rejection of formalism in religion. They cut much deeper.

153. See Käsemann's essay, "The Problem of the Historical Jesus," in *New Testament Questions for Today.*

154. The first seven chapters of Mark are really a redefinition of the word "God."

155. Mark 10:24–27. The point of the story is not a moral exhortation on the evils of wealth. It is rather a statement about how paradoxical the word "power" is, when used of God.

156. Jesus' remarks on children should not be sentimentalized. The point is not that children are innocent, but that they know how to receive a gift—happily and without calculation. See Schweizer, *Good News according to Mark,* on the text in question.

157. When Jesus is made into a religious founder, he is effectively "domesticated"—all kinds of religious practice can be "read back" into him. This had begun even before the New Testament was finished—in fact, even before Mark had finished his Gospel, as the evident community modifications of Jesus' words in Mark 2:20 and 2:28 show.

158. Because the rabbi is, by definition, a commentator on God's law and must unquestioningly accept this law as the mediator and vehicle of the will of God.

159. Again, look for this not in his use of the term "Abba" but in his strange distinction between "my Father" and "your Father."

160. The embarrassment of the homiletic tradition in the face of this text is another indication of the tendency to assimilate Jesus to a tradition which is rather uncritically assumed to begin with him.

161. This Marcan story is also remarkable for the elements which underline Jesus' humanity: he is "deeply moved" and "audibly angered." The act of reaching out to touch the leper (v. 41) seems provocative in the face of the prescriptions of the law.

162. Haenchen in *Der Weg Jesu* argues (against Käsemann) that the story of the baptism is a construction.

163. God is never, for Jesus, the "wholly other" because Jesus is never "outside the divine life, looking in." He is "other" as a partner in dialogue.

164. This is the point of Mark 2:21–22 about the new wine and the patch on the old garment. This statement of the irreconcilability of the new with the old is an interpretation of his remarks on fasting (which immediately precede these).

165. He did this particularly at those moments when, without making

any claim for himself, he redefined the word "God": Mk 2:5, 13–17, 18–20, 23–28; 4:1–8; 7:1–23.

166. This could easily be misunderstood. The answers may be simple and obvious but there is no implication that they are easy. The "simple" answers referred to must contain the substance of the New Testament teaching about Jesus and the substance of what the early councils were trying to preserve. For this reason, these "simple" answers will be profound and inexhaustible. Likewise, the answer "Jesus is a human person" may be obvious to one who takes the Synoptic tradition seriously but this "obvious" answer is one which opens the door to equally profound and metaphysical questions.

167. These terms were favorites of Paul Tillich's. See his *Systematic Theology I.*

168. Gen 1:2.

169. Genesis 1:3–26 presents the word as the vehicle or instrument of creation. Isaiah 55:10 depicts the word of God as similar to the rain and snow which do not return to the place from which they came before they have caused the earth to bring forth new life.

170. It is precisely this which Augustine questioned in his *De Trinitate* 5:10 and 7:7–9.

171. The "ex" in the formula *creatio ex nihilo* (creation from nothing) does not simply mean that something came to be *after* nothing. There was, of course, no material which was used in God's creative act, but nothingness played a role not unlike that played by the material cause in human "creativity." In this sense, the work remains marked by its origin.

172. This is the real meaning of the analogy of being. The act of existence *itself* differs, which can only mean that it differs in degree. This is the basis of Thomas' fourth way and it is this fact which makes it the most powerful of the "proofs" when understood.

173. Hebrews 1:1, in its reference to "God who spoke in diverse ways to our fathers in the prophets," is one of the few explicit references to the Old Testament.

174. See von Rad's interpretation in the volume *Genesis* in the *Westminster Commentary.* Few tendencies are more important than this trend to universalism (which is found at critical points in the J tradition) for the Christian understanding and significance of the Old Testament.

175. Note also the exegetically preferable punctuation of John 1:3b–4a—"what came to be was life in him."
176. This is a good translation of the word which is usually rendered as "justifies." For a fuller treatment, see my notes on "Paul to the Romans" (photo-offset, Moraga, 1977).
177. Justification is the paradoxical exercise of God's *power*. See Käsemann, *New Testament Questions for Today*, "The Righteousness of God in Paul."
178. The post-tridentine manual theology expressed this by speaking of new "terminations" of eternal divine decrees, thus limiting real change to the created world. But if God acts freely, then this limitation cannot be maintained.
179. For the formal rejection of adoptionism, see Denzinger, *Enchiridion Symbolorum*, nn. 310, 314a.
180. Although adoptionism in the formal sense arose in the West, it can be interpreted as the extension to the whole Christ of the Arian doctrine of the creaturely character of the Logos.
181. It is for this reason that the death of Jesus can have cosmic, universal significance. In Jesus, God acts, God becomes, and the world, which exists only in continual dependence on God, is changed in the depths of its being.
182. The ancient Greek concept of history as cyclic is a good illustration of this. The Greek "God" was remote and incapable of participation in worldly existence, and therefore history had no direction, no end, no goal.
183. This statement, so different in form from anything affirmed at Nicaea, is the transposition, into another conceptual framework, of that council's affirmation of the divinity of the Logos.
184. That is, it is the concrete humanity of Jesus which is the sign of the presence of God in the world. See Rahner, *Theological Investigations III*, "The Eternal Significance of the Humanity of Jesus for Our Relationship with God."
185. Certain so-called "neo-Chalcedonian" Christologies in the period before and after World War II tried to take the humanity seriously by creating a kind of human "almost person" in Jesus. Such attempts illustrate one of the principal problems with the unresolved Antiochene elements of the compromise at Chalcedon.
186. There is no trace in the New Testament of dialogue between Jesus and the word or between divine and human "components" in Jesus.

187. This issue has been unnecessarily complicated by later speculation on the "beatific vision" (the face to face knowledge of God
on the part of the blessed in heaven), which a so-called "high"
Christology felt had to be asserted of Jesus. On this, see the
encyclical *Mystici Corporis* of Pius XII (*Acta Apostolicae Sedis* (1943)
215 and the Decree of the Holy Office of June 5, 1918 (Denzinger, *Enchiridion Symbolorum*, n. 2183).

188. That is, any existence other than that which *might be* but *is not*.

189. This is the meaning of Paul's assertion that God chose and called
us in Jesus: Romans 8:29–30.

190. This does not imply that God is derivable, even cognitively, from
the world. The dynamisms of the world reach preliminary fulfillment in man, but at this point it becomes clear that they will be
definitively fulfilled only in the reception of an unmerited gift.

191. Faith is the act of knowing God, but to know a person is not
to objectify that person but rather to accept and affirm the other
in his or her uniqueness. This is what it means to "let the
other be."

192. "Freedom" can mean, on the one hand, the capacity or power to
decide for the truth, and, on the other hand, the actual decision.
The first is freedom in potency and the second is freedom in act.
Freedom is a mystery, but the mystery is not that of *indifference*.
Failure to see this resulted in the Scholastic doctrine that God is
not free in his love of himself.

193. This means that the authority of Chalcedon and other councils
will always be a *derived* authority. Their teaching is binding precisely to the degree to which it protects scriptural doctrine. Conciliar teaching may do this within one set of parameters and fail to
do it within another.

194. An interesting attempt to do this can be found in Gerhard Ebel-
ing's *Introduction to a Theological Theory of Language*.

195. The texts which imply or state this most clearly are probably ones
which were taken over by John and Paul from earlier material—
the Prologue of John's Gospel and Philippians 2:5–11.

196. See the decree of the Council of Chalcedon, Denzinger, *op. cit.*, n.
148.

197. In John, it is the "pre-existence" of the Logos which seems to be
in question, and the Prologue makes at least as much use of
mythology as does Paul in the Philippians text cited above.

198. The scriptural term which is usually translated as "flesh" did not

mean either the body or human nature, but rather the human condition as weak, vulnerable and dependent.

199. Nowhere do the tendencies of the doctrine of the two natures to divide Christ appear more clearly than they do here. Jesus Christ becomes something like the Cartesian "ghost in a machine."

200. The discussion of hypostatic union suggests that there are "things to be united," and this, in turn, drives the Chalcedonian term *physis* another step further away from its original meaning of a principle of growth or activity.

201. The text of Pius XII's encyclical *Humani Generis* should be cited in this connection: "Together with the sources of positive theology, God has given to his Church a living teaching authority to elucidate and explain what is contained in the deposit of faith *only obscurely and implicitly.* . . . If the Church does exercise this function of teaching . . . it is clear how false is a procedure which would *attempt to explain what is clear by what is obscure*" (my italics). The implication is clear: Scripture contains *obscurely* what the teaching authority of the Church presents *lucidly*.

202. In Exodus 3:14 this is stated in terms of God's *name* (the way he was defined for ancient man and put at man's disposal). In the text, God refused to give his name. He "will be the one that" he "will be"—in his own good time and on his own terms.

203. It is difficult to imagine what "good example" could possibly mean under such circumstances, since the conditions under which ordinary human beings must live and act are so different from those which were in vigor for the God-Man.

204. See note 201 above, and note in this connection the essentially defensive, apologetic role accorded (biblical) theology by *Humani Generis:* "It belongs to them (the theologians) to point out how the doctrine of the living teaching authority is to be found either explicitly or implicitly in Scripture and in tradition." The encyclical continues, alluding again to *Inter Gravissimas* of Pius IX: "Hence our predecessor of immortal memory, Pius IX, teaching that the most noble office of theology is to show how a doctrine defined by the Church is contained in the sources of revelation, added these words, and with very good reason, 'in that sense in which it has been defined by the Church.' " This, and the citation in note 201 are taken from paragraph 21 of the NCWC translation of the encyclical *Humani Generis.*

205. This is not to defend the "theology" of (or after) the death of God

which was popular in the late 1960's. This "theology" was a typical fad, whose protagonists showed an amazing ignorance of the tradition of negative theology from Thomas Aquinas to Hegel. The point I wish to make is that the word "God" has often been used to refer to projections of the human mind which (thank God!) do not exist, have no objective reality.

206. This truth could not have been stated at Chalcedon in any other way than the one chosen—that is, by reaffirming the consubstantiality of Logos and God, and affirming that the Logos is the ultimate subject in Jesus Christ.

207. Personhood is, in all dimensions of human experience, the result of dialogue. The person is called into being by the "word" which, in waiting for a response, actually empowers it.

208. See the excursus "das Fleisch" in Kuss, *Der Römerbrief,* 506–540.

209. If not the starting point, at least it was often regarded as the most pressing problem for Scholastic theology to solve. A brilliant example of such an attempt is De La Taille's *Created Actuation by Uncreated Act,* with implications for the theology of grace and of the Spirit, as well as for Christology. Even though the problem solved was a pseudo-problem, achievements like De La Taille's can be transposed into other frameworks and prove useful in more contemporary Christologies.

210. 1 Cor 2:2.

211. 1 Cor 15:14.

212. See Ph. Vielhauer, *Aufsätze zum New Testament,* 1959, 22, and Conzelmann, *Die Apostelgeschichte,* 1963, 187.

213. E. Käsemann, *Jesus Means Freedom,* 1969, 52.

214. Schweizer, *The Good News According to Mark,* 381.

215. *Ibid.,* 381–382.

216. It is this "resurrection theology" which occasioned some of Paul's most important statements on the cross in 1 Corinthians 1 and 2.

217. See Wolfgang Schrage's essay in *Das Kreuz Jesu Christi als Grund des Heils,* Gütersloher Verlagshaus Gerd Mohn, 1968, 51, and also W. Marxsen, "Erwägungen zum Problem des verkündigten Kreuzes," *New Testament Studies* (8), 1961–1962, 204–214.

218. This was probably the meaning of the word "redeemed"; the image of paying a ransom was no longer operative. See Schrage, *op. cit.,* 79.

219. Gal 1:4; 6:14; Rom 8:32.

220. Rom 3:24.

221. 1 Cor 5:7.
222. *Mysterium Salutis 3, 1* (Benziger, 1970), 638.
223. *Ibid.*
224. Huby, *Epître aux Romains.*
225. Schelkle, *Epistle to the Romans,* 40.
226. 1 Cor 2:2.
227. This "boasting" is a recurring theme in 1 Corinthians 1 and 2.
228. 1 Cor 1:24.
229. Rom 8:32.
230. 1 Cor 15:14.
231. 2 Cor 5:19.
232. Rom 5:8.
233. See Bultmann, *Theology of the NT II,* 314–330.
234. Rom 3:25.
235. Rom 3:24.
236. Rom 8:31–32.
237. 1 Cor 1:20.
238. Phil 2:5–11.
239. 1 Cor 1:18.
240. Obviously not in the sense of vengefully or spitefully exulting in man's weakness; the cross remains God's act, not against man but on his behalf. The cross is God's judgment, but the word "judgment" can be used of God only in a most paradoxical sense.
241. Rom 4:17.
242. Phil 2:9.
243. Mk 8:35.
244. Rom 10:4.
245. 1 Cor 1:23.
246. 1 Cor 1:18.
247. Phil 2:9.
248. Schweizer, *op. cit.,* 56.
249. Mk 8:27–33.
250. Mk 1:14–15.
251. Mk 2:7.
252. Schweizer, *op. cit.,* 61.
253. Ernst Käsemann, *Jesus Means Freedom,* 1969, 39.
254. Bornkamm, *Jesus of Nazareth,* 98.
255. Schweizer, *op. cit.,* 174.
256. *Ibid.,* 350.
257. Rom 4:17.

258. All in all, I believe that the "stance" which is described here is a good summary of the substance of religious life, as the various religious orders strive to live it. Admittedly, we human beings have the power to warp and twist almost anything, and we often turn religious life into a barren ascetical wasteland in the name of the cross. We can and ought to be forgiving of such stupidity in ourselves and others, but we also *ought to do something about it.* When we try to do something about it, I believe that a real understanding of the cross (and repeated meditation on 1 Corinthians 1 and 2) will show that the cross, far from being the morbid message of the sufferings we have to bear before being let into glory-land, is a *liberating* event, because it is where we encounter God and where each of us is freed from that most tyrannical and ludicrous of masters—his or her own false self, with its fears, anxieties, pride, pretenses and poses. Religious renewal, whether of the individual or of the institution as such, will not really be effected by adopting one or more of the principles or "insights" of the human potential movement. Some of these are harmless enough; most are simply silly, in an annoyingly pretentious way. Religious life is renewed when those who are committed to it understand it as a special calling to live the Gospel in a peculiarly intense way and realize that the nature of this call and its concrete demands can be grasped only if the Gospel (that is, the entire New Testament) is really understood. Religious life began with this attempt, and as often as it has returned, during its long history, to its scriptural sources, it has thrived and it has shown how indispensable it is to *all* in the Church and to the very life of the Church itself. On the other hand, as often as religious have (almost always unwittingly) substituted human "wisdom" for the word of the cross, the Church has suffered and religious life itself has degenerated into a sterile formalism which substituted nostalgic longing for the often highly romanticized epoch of the "founder" for commitment, in the name of the crucified Lord, to real people and their real problems today. Here (that is, in the effort to achieve renewal of religious life), as in every other task which we face as Christians, there is no substitute for the understanding of that document which is normative for all Christian faith and life—the New Testament. And here it is not the repetition of pious platitudes or the amateurish attempt to find the latest fad of social and political activists in Scripture which will

help. Real piety and authentic renewal will be served by a truly critical and historical understanding of the New Testament proclamation, because this and only this will lead to the Lord Jesus who lives in this proclamation.